# Morphology of Meaning

# Morphology of Meaning
## in the Earliest Indian and European Narrative Discourses

Bhavatosh IndraGuru

DK PRINTWORLD
Publishers of Indian Traditions

**Cataloging in Publication Data — DK**
[Courtesy: D.K. Agencies (P) Ltd. <docinfo@dkagencies.com>]

**Indraguru, Bhavatosh,** 1968- **author.**
Morphology of meaning in the earliest Indian and European narrative discourses / Bhavatosh Indraguru.
pages cm
Includes verses in Sanskrit.

1. Grammar, Comparative and general – Morphology. 2. Discourse analysis, Narrative. 3. Meaning (Philosophy) 4. Panchatantra. 5. Chaucer, Geoffrey, -1400. Canterbury tales. 6. Tipiṭaka. Suttapiṭaka. Khuddakanikāya. Jātaka. 7. Bunyan, John, 1628-1688. Pilgrim's progress. 8. Sanskrit literature – History and criticism. 9. English literature – History and criticism. I. Title.

LCC P241.I53 2018 | DDC 415.9 23

ISBN: 978-81-246-0918-7
First Published in India in 2019


*Printed and published by*:
D.K. Printworld (P) Ltd.
Regd. office : "Vedaśrī", F-395, Sudarshan Park
(ESI Hospital Metro Station), New Delhi - 110015
*Phones* : (011) 2545 3975, 2546 6019
*e-mail* : indology@dkprintworld.com
*Web* : www.dkprintworld.com

*To my mother*

Smt. Kamla IndraGuru

# Preface

NARRATIVE is, by far, the most complete expression of an artistic situation, in that it composes and constructs the reality in truth and truth in identity, and, on that account, it sums up all the paradoxes and contradictions inherent in the experiences of life. It would mean, therefore, that the growth of narrative is comprehended on both sides of the scale where vertical and horizontal axes converge along a point of intersection. The remarkable consolidation of a situation similar to this is observed in the primacy of correlation between the sets of objects, chain of events, situations and the like occurring in either the homogeneous experiences or diametrically opposed heterogeneous situations. In either of the cases, there is a necessary transmutation of the events that anticipates the creation of refined orders of meaning in the form of conjunction, injunction, conception, inception and comprehension. The impression of the situation bears a consequence of assertion almost to the extent of universality in Indian and Western narrative traditions, and, for that matter, the earliest narratives like *Pañcatantra*, *Hitopadeśa*, *Kathāsaritsāgara*, *Baitāl Paccīsī*, *Siṁhasana Battīsī*, *The Decameron*, *Legends of King Arthur*, *The Canterbury Tales*, *Aesop's Fable* and *The Pilgrim's Progress*, meaning primarily is revealed in the recognition and approval of a concentrated personality that is authoritatively the foundation of narrativization of characters, action and the whole discourse. It is to be understood that narrative action in the *Pancatantra* is almost expansive whereas European narratives explicate the variants of narrative through the reduction of the contents. The methodologies which are specific to the narratives of India and the West confer a mark of authority on the conduct of character, the extent of signification and the richness of discursive intentions in accordance with the consummation of cultural tradition specific to each, yet the conduct of meaning upholds the manner of qualitative enrichment precisely outlined in ethical and moral universality inherent in the categorical inscription. This study, therefore, proposes to lay a foundation for construction of a theory of meaning in relation to the action that is obtained in the progress of earliest narratives at large.

# Contents

# Introduction

THE manifestation of artistry in the earliest narrative discourses is explicit and, therefore, the contents are exposed to the external environment by a number of associative events, of which, addition and multiplication are the most important. An action in these earliest narratives acquires fullness by the virtue of semblance to the wholeness of the form. Every action commences at the note of the creation of an individual/character/form/event and the progression is such that there is a consistency in obtaining full-length realization of the given situation. It is thus the definition of earliest narratives approximates to the creation of those purposeful events which have the wholeness executed in the resolution of an object into event, even otherwise, event into object. This is to prove the point that reversibility has a thoroughgoing expression for itself in this scheme of the representation of the situation. Indian and Western traditions have been, since the antiquity, and, of which, Indian tradition has assuredly a methodology of conceiving and composing order in a framework for such discourse. *Pañcatantra*, being the earliest narrative in the human civilization, brings about the significant revelation with regard to the nature and significance of the individual and the corresponding actions. Following *Pañcatantra* in Indian tradition, we have *Hitopadeśa, Jātakakathāvalī, Kathāsaritsāgara, Betāl Paccīsī, Siṁhāsana Battīsī.* Similarly, on the Western side, there are equally important works of such nature primarily *Aesop's Fables, Legends of King Arthur, The Decameron, The Canterbury Tales, The Pilgrim's Progress*, etc. These are the ones in which we can have a complete artistic situation entailing fulfilment of figural and formal actions. In the narratives belonging to these two traditions, both the construction of the character and the configuration of an action, have remarkably the idealized perspectives. In each, the nature of action is very realistic hence it commutes itself through its orientation in the cause and the effect. The dimension of this dichotomy acquires various meanings and internalizations. In Indian situation, the action is almost entirely reversible, thus it foresees the growth of cumulative assortment of events. The order of one event is such that it always revives and restores itself in the other and the succession of the similar events continues till the final resolution. In *Pañcatantra*, for example, the individual and characters respond to each other via representative and functional codes and the enlargement of these codes is so much so that the effect of reversibility becomes ordained even otherwise in the adoption of the relative roles. This could be seen as one of the greatest technical advancements that brings a complete methodology of transformation. It so happens that the animal character and the human figures come to terms by discovering the equivalence and correlatives for swapping their roles. This is the way in which compatibility of the signifier is achieved and brought forth. In *Pañcatantra*, the principles which have brought about the conduct of the situation have similarly restored the incarnation of one into the other. It would mean that every character is capable of creating an index and the stability of the index is apparent in almost all the forms in which a character enjoys strength and commitment. The situation is sustained equally well in *Kathāsaritsāgara*, *Jātakakathāvalī*, *Betāl Paccīsī* and *Siṁhāsana Battīsī*. In the earliest European narratives, the organization of an action is obtained in an event that is, by and large, irreversible in nature. It allows us to understand the qualification of differential perception in the characters. The index that has been created in each of the characters bears the strength of his/her individuality and thus it does not enter into any correspondences whatsoever with any other character. In other words, we can say that the character is not reinvented in the other, consequently the progression as such does not come to be inscribed. In the *Legends of King Arthur*, *The Decameron*, *The Canterbury Tales* and others, excellence as such is always specified in a particular circumstance that deals only with the beginning and the end of the event concerned and, as a rule, follows the creation of meaning randomly at the various events. One does not necessarily follow the other and the entire configuration of the action in *The Canterbury Tales* observes the principle of exclusion in which the individuality of character is primarily significant in that it does not allow the subordinate event to come up and invent the procedure of change. The Knight, the Squire, the Doctor, Wife of Bath, Summoner, Pardoner and others suggest an extraordinarily high degree of exclusion through which they substantiate their own individualities all along. Boccaccio's *The Decameron* further brings about a comprehensive formation of a realistic model in which compunctious exclusion of ideological framework in the character suffers from a loss of a habit – habit that is revealed in the exercise of one powerful motive. The character expresses him or her by obtaining certain degree of proficiency in conflicting desire as a basic motive. In desire itself the point of view of the character is contained, thus he/she lives or dies till the time desire and its minor variants like greed, or, even otherwise, temptation has strength to construct and coordinate a system of profit and loss. Nearly, every human emotion like love, hate, union, separation, joy, delight and the like comes to be determined. On account of such an exercise of pursuit, it would definitely approximate to the following formula:

$$\sum = A = A^{-}.$$

In this, progression and regression are having equal projection; accordingly, each projection is also, at the same time, definitely a point in regression. As it happens in the formulation cited above, the obvious consequence of the characteristic of such a sort stilts the growth of a character as larger, bigger and higher opportunities are found to be not consistent with the world view contained in the given character. Every male character in *The Decameron* has a motive to confirm the sense of his material prosperity and every woman consequently has an intention to be the medium for the achievement of all the immediate necessities. This is essentially the formation that has been virtuously engrained in the characteral form. This would amount to say that purpose is the motive and strength of the character, yet the purpose is so keenly intervened by the self-interest in that it loses its universal significance. We can understand that the purpose is mutated in the impersonal ethics of the characters that does not allow them to enlarge the comprehension of life, nature and the world. In *The Pilgrim's Progress* and other works of such nature, characters rise and fall only through vertical elevations in which aims and ambitions are, by and large, assuredly contrastive. Repeated contrast brings about gradual reduction, and reduction in its being prepares the way for annihilation. In *The Pilgrim's Progress*, Christian's problems are certainly the ethico-moral inversion that forces him to stand in opposition to himself and exercise of opposition gradually disembodies the strengthening of the function of virtue. It would seem that every meaning constructed in the narratives is precisely on such evidence of manifestation.

## II

The pursuit of meaning in Indian and European earliest narratives is to convey the action by certain instruments of transformation of which, conjunction, injunction, conception and inception are the most important. Instances of such sorts are abundant in *Pañcatantra*, *Hitopadeśa*, *Kathāsaritsāgara* and the like. In *Pañcatantra*, the degree and kind of reinvention is brilliant and amazing, and, on this account, animal forms and human characters both distinctly occupy their places in specific locale of the time and correspondence is so effective that every step forward becomes its reappearance in the next/higher level of existence. It is noteworthy to find out the similarity of codes identified in emphatic relationship between these two orders of characters. It would also assuredly suggest that contents are so super-cultivated that the assertions at once become pragmatic and thoroughly rationalized. This ability to perceive sensibly is an achievement of the narrative enjoined upon *Pañcatantra* and others. It is not at all the matter of only proposing the set of correlatives from the prospective decipherment rather it is an ability to reinvent oneself in the significance of a cultivated form that brings forth the universality of the characters. In *Pañcatantra*, the logic of narrative events is communicated through graduated signifiers in which every event is worthy of being suggested, and the term of communication sustains a potential of both the linguistic and emotive forms. From the point of view of methodology, every discourse so generated approaches a development through the evolution in which both the structure and function at every instance acquire newness and precision. Even within the contrastive illustrations of authenticated identity, we are sure to find out that the sensibility begets the strength of logic not to be found elsewhere.

In the Western situation, the correspondence between the essence and existence of the characters develops situational urgency, accordingly, every character/event/form finds a worthy application only in relation to the impending reality. Predominance of reality and excess of rationality are obviously the significant structures which bring about order and strength to them. It would be interesting to note that the manner of characteral modification in relation to the context and medium is appropriately very different in Indian and Western conditions. In Indian situation, stay of an experience is to the extent of indivisibility, secured on account of repeated reversibility. While in equivalent Western perspective, permanence and infinity are logically antedated through a more secure and affirmative stay in the necessary reality. It would seem to be quite pertinent to offer the contention that the continuity of modification in resolving identity into value suggests both empirical and rational variants in narrative discourses, and, while it obtains resolute affirmation with a graduated yet shortened progression, it really doesn't carry any excellence both in relation to value and meaning. The ability to signify a variation by opting for a committed change through experience and the language finds out its first remarkable expression in conjunction. Conjunction is appropriately a suggestive instrument that brings about equivalence between the external and internal artistic environments in which the character happens to have his or her stay. In the earliest Indian narratives, the condition is extraordinary and unique in that the semblance does not constitute a mark of differentiation or assertion, rather it immediately and forthwith brings about a new variant of the character. This shift, merger, coalescence, recreation and infusion of object into event marks and identifies period of growth in the character himself/

herself. The other instruments of modification, which similarly play a role in proposing a complete range of resolutions and approach refinement, are injunction, conception and inception. The figural form and ratiocinated identity both enter into a complete correspondence. It is because of this that the actions achieve fullness and diversity of various sorts and kinds. In European system, the identification of action and the event becomes severally distinct, and thus, the extent and degree of realization by an action of the event, event of the object, and object of the subject remain only distinguished by the virtue of their own universals. It is in that way the separation between the value of an individual and the meaning of action becomes indiscreet and to an extent incoherent. In *The Decameron*, *Legends of King Arthur*, *The Canterbury Tales*, *The Pilgrim's Progress* and *Aesop's Fables* the development of character is independent of the growth of action, consequently, there is a substantiation of irreversibility. In these cases correspondence is intended to be obtained.

The question of meaning, and consequently the structure and function of meaning in the earliest Indian and European narratives, is a fact or rule or law that governs the ethos of artistry that is purported to be created. The work of this nature in which the emphasis is mainly laid on explicating the terms of configuration, exchange, change and modification of the contents, constructs and categories that participate in various processes leading finally to the emergence of universal in the form of meaning, the participation and sympathy of the reader would be called for yet, however, it is believed that this work would fill in the vacuum just because nothing much has so far been done in this area.

The index of identity and the content of reality are situationally best ordered in the extent of meaning that is created as a rule when the object and the subject are formalized into each other. The advent of concept in consequence of a conceptualization of such sort amounts to the beginning of a larger process of value presentation accordingly gives rise to individual action and discourse depending upon the extent to which the change has been introduced. The first remarkable consequence of such brevity of contents is felt in the growth of the narratives. In the same way, the historical tradition of narratives draws upon a greater and bigger representation of a significant experience in the earliest narratives of Indian and Western traditions. In these narratives, the mechanics of conception of the character, action and discourse anticipate a complete realization of simultaneous events bearing the designation in the form of object and subject. The narrative object and the narrative subject comprehend a possibility of renewing the exchange supplementing the ideologies and constructing an inversion of attitudes with the help of explicated variants, which lie in the conventional as well as an immediate environment. In fact, there is a kind of precision that invests a simulation by enlarging the reinvention of context, content and medium. The evolving contents within these designated categories give rise to refined hierarchy of meaning which in turn is manifest in five principal forms, namely, conjunction, injunction, conception, inception and comprehension. Each of these is so well observed in *Pañcatantra, Hitopadeśa, Kathāsaritsāgara, Betāl Paccīsī, Siṁhāsana Battīsī, The Decameron, Aesop's Fables, The Canterbury Tales* and *The Pilgrim's Progress*. There cannot be any denying of the fact that the intensity of experience or otherwise of only category that proposes itself as a compulsive model on the character or the event or the situation, directly resolves the situation in the direction of an ideal form through which the action of these narratives is determined. In this regard, it would be worthwhile to understand that complete familiarity, total identification, exact correspondence and unquestionable similarity between the refined contents of categories involved in the actions of the narratives, which bring forth complete transformation, and, as we have suggested earlier, conjunction, along with other types of meanings, are born. Such an extraordinary event of necessity induces the aspect of universality that has been one of the confirmed reasons for the perpetuation of these narratives beyond time and beyond ages.

The present study would therefore offer certain conceptual structures, which would determine the propriety of a new theoretical effort in this direction. While certain classics like Vladimir Prop's *Morphology of the Folk Tale* and A.J. Greimas'

*On Meaning: Selected Writings in Semiotic Theory* have their own importance, yet a full-length and full-bodied account of meaning due upon the narrative actions in these narratives has not been so far attempted on comparative principles. It is hoped, on such an account, that this book would certainly strengthen the state of letters in the same direction.

# 1

# Conjunction

## I

Narrative is a constitution of purposeful events in which action is intended as a prospect of full-scale and full-length assertion and comprehension, for that matter, it becomes an event of reorganization, reinvention and recreation of an experience in which object, subject, cause, effect, appearance and reality are primarily involved. In each, assortment of time as an attitude, motive, aptitude and commitment is made permanent by fixation. Action in narrative is determined through the set(s) or group(s) of characters who transform themselves into the models of expression in accordance with facility made in reorganization of a given artistic situation. It would mean that narrative is a comprehensive interaction of object-location, subject-creation and time-distribution through a proper convergence of attending situations. It is for this reason that in earliest narratives, there is a movement of object and subject in which both are reinvented and reorganized on a timescale and converge along a figuration that is linear, cyclical, oblong or even oblique. What is primarily established is the experience of individual forms that gather and transmute themselves into recurrent models of richness and universality. The manner of conducting an action in the narrative is by dividing it into immediate and extended situations yet, in either cases, strength of action comes from a centralized object, figure or an individual who borrows the determinants from an environment immediate to him or from conjunctions gathered in inhibited or uninhibited consciousness. In a narrative, action intends and suggests a completion at the point at which it was initiated, hence objects, forms and characters develop ideal terms for identification through the extreme of conformity (warmth, involvement, understanding and the like) and distance of nonconformity (grudge, hatred, ill will, rage and the like). Indian and European narratives like *Pañcatantra, Hitopadeśa, Kathāsaritsāgara, Jātakakathāvalī, Betāl Paccīsī, Siṁhāsana Battīsī, Aesop's Fables, The Decameron, The Canterbury Tales, The Pilgrim's Progress* and the like create composite situations and coherent terms of evaluation. In each, the characteral evolution and thematic universalization are almost entirely complete, thus the ground of comparison and analysis is thoroughly justified.

## II

Meaning in the narrative is formally an appropriate measure of changing an event into a resolution, and, for the purpose, different shades, aspects and facets of object, form – individual or any other form of action – within the given sequence of action interact with the projection of motive, manner, ideas, conviction, attitude and perception whose relative worth is sometimes only to supervise. It is in that way, we come across a situation in which figural forms (object and individual) work out a scheme of option (or fulfilment) through a choice to put up a necessity of strength directly or in the events of assertion. Methods of obtaining meaning in any specific/ideal situation would invariably be the following:

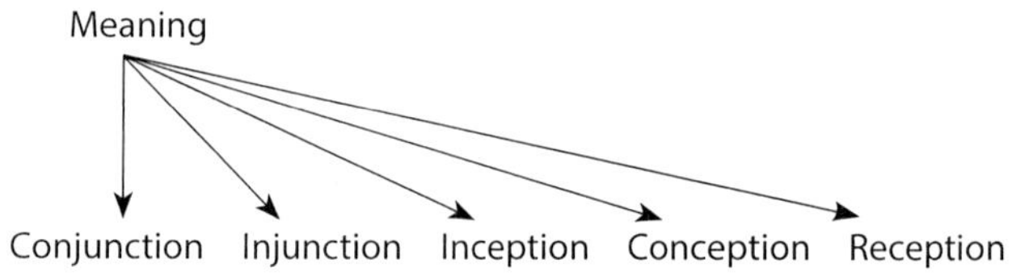


In this, the situation will have the following explanation and work of each constituent is affected through a typical formative excellence:

> Conjunction: Method through which the purpose of association is finally established.
>
> Injunction: Definite style of upholding the worth of absolute individual experience.
>
> Inception: Revival of a necessity to restore the motive of organization.

Conception: Acceptance of primary, secondary, natural or synthetic facets of terms of life.

Reception: Convergence of the whole into whole.

It must be accepted that nearly all the conditions, circumstances, relations and assertions within the narrative commit themselves to the acts of synthesis and organization brought about by these five different orders of resolution of an object into an event. The scale of meaning adopts an idea of notion/comprehension through purpose/function inherent upon character form(s). Indian and Western narratives have distinct strengths which could be identified through the following scheme(s):

**Indian Narratives**

- Character-Action Term (regular growth into models)
- Concept (ideal, real, concrete, truth, primary)
- Evolution (universal)
- Dimension of the subject (functional)

**European Narratives**

- Character-Action Dimension (non-functional, aberrated)
- Term (indefinite, linear and irreversible)
- Concept (illusory, enraged and secondary)
- Evolution (local, situational and occasional)

Structure of meaning and emergence of manifold strength of individual/object/form in the narrative uphold the validity of both the terms. Meaning, so to say, is the strength of character in its correspondence and is surely a realistic model to upgrade enormity found in each of the actions. The figure of correspondence that enacts a necessity of forming constituents of organization is fixed up in accordance with suitability of initiating an experience in organic/inorganic system in a character/object/form and proposal obtained through upcoming versions of sensible model.

## III

In narrative discourses, the propriety of assimilation and recognition of the corresponding term, strength or situation is made with a view to suggest the manner of object-strength or purpose of subject-motivation towards approval and acceptance. The basis of construction is normally indicated in the attitudinal assertion of characters and individuals. A character sustains himself/ herself with a primary need of prolonging his/her stay in any course of event, for that matter, he/she collects evidence of nearly all the benefits that might accrue on account of this association. An individual/object/a form is situated in the wider formation, accordingly, in the first place, he occupies an empirical strength created by the virtue of his stay in consciousness and conscience, and, second, his/her stretch is worth the accommodation to external material conduct. In each, he is supposed to have equated and cumulated, multiplicated and relative points of enrichment and excellence of his/her own experience. This manner of establishing a code of concept, comprehension and logic in which there is a grand association of nearly all the modes of external and internal terms is exactly the logic involved in the making of conjunction evidently a term for meaning.

The circumstances that enable an individual/object/a subject to conjunct the occasion of extremely convenient and altogether difficult events in which there is a definite separation of equivalent forms bring about the manner of its outward illustration through the characteristics that are incorporated into its formal features. There is no other way of saying that an individual/object/a form in a narrative purpose is a dispensation through an activity that he/ she does in the final position, obtained in each such stretch of event formation. There is no compulsion as such to either concentrate or heighten or make compulsive the time formation. There are two different ways to explain the nature of this synthesis in a narrative projection. In the first place, there is no limit that is put on the expansion of the strength of the character, and, second, immediate limit of opening relation in respect of a character is extraordinarily concrete. The individual/object/form makes the beginning, and the beginning is normally proposed as a principle to identify, hence, it merits the identity with a strong display of warmth. The beginning itself is a proposal to initiate habit in the conduct so as to offer an internalization of the right direction purported to be created by the same. In the face of this form of character formation in the narratives, the characters have a rather free hand in the exercise of the choices – to either commute credentials underlying the choice of entering into stretch of fellow object and subject. The motive appears to be exactly to permit the formation of a function in the lengthened series of extension. The earliest assumption of an individual/object/a form with regard to one's own projection through equivalents, symbols, prolonged object or flat utterance is a way to incline necessary norms in developing the rationality. It is also necessary to understand how the different parts of concept cohere and compose differences in the working of the structures underway – the actual process through which any form is accepted to survive in this large and wide world. The evidence of such a fact may be intended as a measure of function/object/individual. Conjunction is a form of equative proposition that is imminently strengthened in the generative form of the object. Equalizing circumstances come forth when the external forms brought about by either free accessibility or compulsive assortment come up, therefore, generation of normal vision makes out an experience at the seeming external level, and, intention to reform the weaker instinct through which one sees one's fall in the time of life are the two strong cases where equative forms are created and begotten. In a restive form that opts for a development beyond the earlier described system, there will have to be a need to intercept a coordinate or an equation. Nevertheless to equate is to align and to align is to correlate and to correlate is to transform and to transform is to synthesize and to synthesize is, in turn, to equate. For that matter, equation is a necessary means to restore the meaning of generated part of personality in the stretch of an individual and expansion of correlated form. The utterance made by an individual/object form is open for immediate internalization through its cumulative and relative proposition and magnitude, obtained in either asymmetrical or symmetrical formation. It would mean that any organization of form in a narrative event would opt for inclusion through the necessity and future prospects, therefore, we are generally invited to attend extreme of the situation in which enrichment of formal objects coincides with its projection through the orientation of sensibility in the external space. This method is for exposing the extended, imminent and realistic content/category/construct in local as well as universal artistic set-ups. While we pursue an ideal for this, we can form an opinion to the effect that narrative is composed and conceived when conjunctive appropriation is invariably inherent in the natural method of any progressive event.

### IV

In Indian and European narrative discourses, for example, *Pañcatantra*, *Hitopadeśa*, *Jātakakathāvalī*, *Kathāsaritsāgara*, *Betāl Paccīsī*, *Siṁhāsana Battīsī*, *The Decameron*, *The Pilgrim's Progress*, *The Canterbury Tales*, *Legends of King Arthur*, *Aesop's Fables*, *The Arabian Nights* and the like, application of conjunction receives authentic, refined and concrete instances, and, for that matter, conjunction becomes an instrument to revive the coherence, synthesis and organization of the multiplicative function to determine the form of characteral network. The action that is finally turned as recourse to function in enhancing merit of the same action is supposedly primary extension of conjunction motives. On the one hand, there is a large recognition of growing individual/object/form, and, on the other, there is also an adaptability of this manner of formation of virtual others of the system. In Indian narrative discourses, conjunction is an act of developing all the major forms of existence through speech, accent, or utterance regulation. It is because of this, the action assumes a reception into the formal structure and form, where the interrelationship between object and subject is normally established. Such strength seems to be hidden in the consolidation of experience and enrichment of language that the action presupposes or foresees. It is not that by making speech, the work of content is opened for the sight of observer at random, and at once. It is, on the other hand, a committed proposition to make the resultant of enormous speed at which the objects in the narrative are conceiving their transformation. This leads to an analysis of the fact that harmony of change and movement of reception of the character into an event are altogether different equations involved in this proposition. In *Pañcatantra*, *Hitopadeśa*,

*Jātakakathāvalī*, *Kathāsaritsāgara* and the like, we are invited to attend the fact that observable contents and achieved construction of a meaning are normally the first principle that the situation/ events in the narrative allow. There can be no activity against the renewal or formation of strength in the action of the system, it leads to perceptual comprehension. In *Pañcatantra*, the purpose of composing an alliance with partner or the fellow being is given a native form in which objects/individuals meet so as to fulfil the wants and approve the conduct of one another. The art of looking with an eye of observation and comprehending the extension of interrelationship is a groundwork that extends the system of life and space through generally a wider compass. In *Pañcatantra*, the act of narration is itself a plan to recommend oneself into the receptive circle of the next object/individual. For example, look at the following:

> भो दमनक, श्रृणाषि शब्दं दूरान्महान्तम् । सोऽब्रवीत् – 'स्वामिन् श्रृणोमि । ततः किम् ।' पिंगलक आह – 'भद्र अहमस्माव्दनाद् गन्तुमिच्छामि ।' दमनक आह – 'कस्मात् ।' पिंगलक आह – 'यतोऽधास्मव्दने किमप्यपूर्व सत्त्वं प्रविष्टं यस्यायं महाशब्दः श्रूयते । तस्य च शब्दानुरूपेण पराक्रमेण भाव्यम् । इति । दमनक आह – यच्छव्दमात्रादपि भयमुपगतः स्वामी, तदप्ययुक्तम् ।
>
> *bho damanaka, śṛṇāṣi śabdaṁ dūrānmahāntam* । *so 'bravīt – 'svāmin śṛṇomi* । *tataḥ kim* ।*' piṅgalaka āha – 'bhadra ahamasmāvdanād gantumicchāmi* ।*' damanaka āha – 'kasmāt* ।*' piṅgalaka āha – 'yato 'dhāsmavdane kimapyapūrva sattvaṁ praviṣṭaṁ yasyāyaṁ mahāśabdaḥ śrūyate* । *tasya ca śabdānurūpeṇa parākrameṇa bhāvyam* । *iti* । *damanaka āha – yacchavdamātrādapi bhayamupagataḥ svāmī, tadapyayuktam* ।
>
> – *Pañcatantra*, Mitrabheda, p. 33

In this remarkable utterance, we can understand how the inventions of external correlatives develop an assertion and inquisition that are normally not found in the growth of sensible terms and objects. Damanaka and Piṅgalaka are conveniently located in an absolutely synthesized situation. The apprehension of one is inquisition of another and inquisition of another is commenced in the external motives of the other. In this way, there is a formation of relation of faith inviting the conduct of sensibility and experience for the purposeful sanctity of whole system. The manner of externalizing the exhortation is in the spirit of bold proclamation of reason and this reason is as extensive as any content that is no fear as such and there is only an engagement in the very foundation of apprehension. This is, perhaps, the difference between the Indian and the Western narrative traditions. This difference really cultivates the idea that homocentric forms containing an idea of distance and apprehension appear in Indian narratives as matters verified through objects inhering in the vicinity of resolution. For example, look at the following:

> भो दमनक, श्रृणाषि शब्दं दूरान्महान्तम् । सोऽब्रवीत् - 'स्वामिन् श्रृणोमि ।'
>
> *bho damanaka, śṛṇāṣi śabdaṁ dūrānmahāntam* । *so 'bravīt – 'svāmin śṛṇomi* ।*'* – *Pañcatantra*, Mitrabheda, p. 33

Illusory perception generates negotiations through a consolidation, while still retaining a firm hold on reality. The internalization of reality through the facts promoted as external universal commences immediate attention. That is why when Damanaka inquires into the arrangement of supra-motives, he manages to control the context of evidences, for that matter, he secures progression of committed terms. The evidence of multiplying assertions upholds validity of contemplating a solid groundwork for revival of conjunction. It has to be understood that conjunctions induct nearly all known variation in attitudes and expressions. In *Hitopadeśa*, for example, consequence of evolving this attitude through an approximately degenerate background becomes, in turn, of whole imaginative ideal embedded in the action:

> तदत्र सरसि स्नात्वा सुवर्णकङ्कणं गृहाण । ततो यावदसौ तव्दच:प्रतीतो लोभात्सर: स्नातुं प्रविशति तावन्महापटे निमग्र: पलायितुमक्षम: । पटे पतितं दृष्ट्वा व्याघ्रोऽवदत् - 'अहह, महापटपतितोऽसि । अतस्त्वामहमुत्थापयामि ।' इत्युक्त्वा शनै: शनैरूपगम्य तेन व्याघ्रेण धृत:, स पान्थोऽचिन्तयत् इति चिन्तयन्नेवासौ: व्याघ्रेण व्यापादित: खादितश्च। अतोऽहं ब्रवीमि - ''कङ्कणस्य तु लोभेन'' इत्यादि । अत: सर्वथाऽविचारितं कर्म न कर्तव्यम् ।
>
> *tadatra sarasi snātvā suvarṇakaṅkaṇaṁ gṛhāṇa* । *tato yāvadasau tavdacaḥpratīto lobhātsaraḥ snātuṁ praviśati tāvanmahāpaṭe nimagraḥ palāyitumakṣamaḥ* । *paṭe patitaṁ dṛṣṭvā vyāghro 'vadat – 'ahaha, mahāpaṭapatito 'si* । *atastvāmahamutthāpayāmi* ।*' ityuktvā śanaiḥ*

*śanairūpagamya tena vyāghreṇa dhṛtaḥ, sa pāntho 'cintayat iti cintayannevāsauḥ vyāghreṇa vyāpāditaḥ khāditaśca* । *ato 'haṁ bravīmi – "kaṅkaṇasya tu lobhena" ityādi* । *ataḥ sarvathā 'vicāritaṁ karma na kartavyam* ।

–*Hitopadeśa*, p. 18

Here we can contemplate a situation in which empirical conjunctions build up strength of multiple variations within the artistic form, therefore, objects stay even at the maturity of a noteworthy meaning. There is a continuity of transformation of object into external form determining the worth of subject, in this context, as a Wayfarer (*pathika*). The extension of such a scheme of committed conjunction is evident in the fact that speech does not establish any informal alliance between innocent and decrepit models rather it conducts in-depth inquiry into such situations as to how genitive formations like (conviction, trust, faith and hope) could be made thoroughly permanent and continuous. The question of constituting a set of perception to have a method for attitudes and sensation come to be established as proposal for progress, growth and space in external system of universe. The Lion (*vyāghra*) and Wayfarer (*pathika*) both establish a continuity and permanence for strengthening inquisition and inherent curiosity, and, each is stabilized for the sake of perpetual faith and trust. The rage of Lion as symbol of functional formation and order completes equations leading to curious inception on the part of Wayfarer who resorts to various persuasions for his claims regarding authoritative and incomplete distribution of half-formed contents in him. The logic of obtaining an equation is brought to further conviction through ineffective display of interrogative potential in the Wayfarer. Sequences of interrogation by Wayfarer are not completely manipulated through wisdom of either sensibility or even perception. His greed in finding a readymade solution to the form of an equation makes him succumb and Lion takes precedence over the contentions involved in reason, rationality and ratiocinative enactments. This proves the point that an activity temporarily mounted on fractional inputs (greed, lust, rage, avarice and desire) hopelessly disobeys the synthesis of action and inaction while itself invites a complete reaction. In either of these persuasive forms, credibility of Wayfarer as a respondent is never thoroughly established. This brings us to an important question for comprehension and valuation. The question invariably is – what is the groundwork of formative principle attitude, sensibility and thoughts in the narrative discourse? The formative contents are generated through a visual perception of affordable action or inaction, and, in either case, immediate strength adds to effective extension of attending form. Attitude is a necessary requirement for the direct involvement into a continuous experience hence it occasions a formulation of pragmatic utterance/speech in such a way that chance of free movement into next experience is possible. For example, look at the following:

> उपकोशामथाभ्यर्थ्य राज्ञा त्वतिकुतूहलात् ।
> सदस्युद्घाटिता तत्र मञ्जूषा स्फोटितार्गला ।।
>
> निष्कृष्टास्तेऽपि पुरूषास्तमः पिण्डा इव त्रयः ।
> कृच्छाच्च प्रत्यभिज्ञाता मन्त्रिभिर्भूभृता तथा ।।
>
> *upakośāmathābhyarthya rājñā tvatikutūhalāt* ।
> *sadasyudṛghāṭitā tatra mañjūṣā sphoṭitārgalā* ।।
>
> *niṣkṛṣṭāste 'pi purūṣāstamaḥ piṇḍā iva trayaḥ* ।
> *kṛcchācca pratyabhijñātā mantribhirbhūbhṛtā tathā* ।।
>
> – *Kathāsaritsāgara*, p. 46

Here the character stands in between the event and resolution, and has a fair stay in the each. She (Upakośa) conceives an action through hospitality of motives on either side of her existence. Precisely, there is an ineffective, infirm, enfeebled and weak function of the subject. Three male characters that are pursuing Upakośa to demotivate the alliance of conformity that moves upside and dissolves into major forms of abstraction. For example, lady (Upakośa) is approached by three different male forms in which the strength of idea is weak and hollow and does not bear the mark of any noteworthy generosity. In the context related to Lion and the Wayfarer, we can understand that formative principles are unquestionably mounted on curious affirmation through interrogative function. The object (Wayfarer) and the subject (Lion) insert credit ethos in the subject hence receive the sanction of figure of addition. Inquisition confirms an attitude to permanence and thinking becomes an act of ensuring a place in the time and space, therefore, subject could transform even a random and fragmentary motion, consequently, relative forms build up emotive/content categorization so as to effectively bring about poise and balance. For example, any standardized situation, constituted on behalf of such, shall bear the following poise/balance formula:

| | | |
|---|---|---|
| Experience | - | Qua Experience |
| Thought | - | Significant Thought |
| Language | - | Enriched Language |

The speech, thus, produced in an act of narrative will communicate internal and external forms through inhibited inhabitation and exhorted exhibition and assure us of direct progression in which individual/object/form would be placed at the middle and universal absolute at tertiary level hence we will have:

Individual ⟶ Soul ⟶ Universe

Basic attitude that develops acts of formation of ethos is intentionally acquired merit of conjunction and reveals as to how character/form composes codes for alignment. The Wayfarer and Lion both opt for indefinite circulation on a half-closing and half-expanding circle hence approach of both is co-extensive and co-terminus and there comes a time when movement is become specific to ensure a negotiation through which content of action (acquisition of gold/grab of prey) is enriched. Let's have a look at the following:

> प्रकाशं ब्रूते – 'कुत्र तव कटणम्?' व्याघ्रो हस्तं प्रसार्य दर्शयति । पान्थोऽवदत् – 'कथं मारात्मके त्वयि विमसः?' । व्याघ्र उवाच 'शृणु रे पान्थ! प्रागेव यौवनदशायामतिदुर्वत्त आसम् । अनेकगोमानुषाणां वधान्मे पुत्र मृता दाराश्च ।
>
> *prakāśaṁ brūte – 'kutra tava kaṭaṇam?' vyāghro hastaṁ prasārya darśayati । pāntho 'vadat – 'kathaṁ mārātmake tvayi vimasaḥ?'। vyāghra uvāca – 'śṛṇu re pāntha! prāgeva yauvanadaśāyāmatidurvatta āsam । anekagomānuṣāṇāṁ vadhānme putra mṛtā dārāśca ।*
>
> – *Hitopadeśa*, p. 15

Wisdom, in the situation, is an act of attitude, therefore, it is neither recognized through conditions nor even through imposition – it is worked out through persuasion that primarily conceives a term for largest comprehension of sensibility. Decrepit and degenerate instinct immediately and abruptly conducts an association that is how Lion (offering a golden ring so as to facilitate his release/ rescue from the mire) and Wayfarer (greedy yet innocent) finds an opportunity to have a discourse. The association explains the nature of perfect competition that is exactly homogenized. The Lion and Wayfarer become participants in a natural composition whose situations are properly and really subjective in nature. There is a precedence of emotion over will and attitude; over idea hence strength of composition compensates unavailability of exact and opposite terms. Lion begins by saying *śṛṇu re pāntha* meaning thereby that invitation to formally associate does not extend the fine network of reasonable assessment and leads to both persuasion and imposition. There is a persuasion in which Lion has to extend himself and retain the symbolical position of a ruler and devise ways to hopeful terms to the Wayfarer so that conjunction in reality is achieved. We can assume that the object (Wayfarer) and the subject (Lion) invent an action that appears to be initiated and completed by them severally and each. Essential structure of conjunction depends much on how the object and the subject interpose constitution of immediate form looming large on them. Action of the Lion is imminent in the context of his own survival. If he does not act, he would not be in a position to survive, therefore, acting is a preparatory exercise to unfold a code for the revival into the system of existence and the Wayfarer is only a dull messenger, who receives an exposition without even recycling necessary urge of curiosity. The sequence presented by this narrative is circumstantial, situational and universal in as much as action on the part of Lion and Wayfarer is intended through a process of selection, and choice over the preference is kept minimum.

## V

The appearance of models of conjunction anticipates building up reliable strength in both thinking and perception. In thinking, the conjunctive situation is in a state of extension so as to group nearly all the categories of comprehension and there is no composition as such for the excellence of external motive. It is out and out an inwardly located process, while, on the other side, failure (in conjunction) restores the method of formation of hard and bright constituent of judgemental formation. In that way resultant action unquestionably relies more on mental form than on anything else. In *The Decameron,* action proposes a commitment toward conjunction by opening it on account of multiplication. Look at the following:

> Alas! why take I not my pleasure whom I may, seeing that I never need a lack for occasions of trouble and vexation of spirit? Here is a fair wench, and no one in the world to know. If I can bring her to pleasure me, I know not why I should not do so. Who will know? No one will ever know; and sin that is hidden is half forgiven; this chance may never come again; so, methinks, it were the part of wisdom to take the boon which God bestows. So musing, with an altogether different purpose from that with which he had come, he drew near the girl, and softly bade her to be comforted . . . came at last to show her what he would be at.
>
> – Boccaccio 1951: 43

The characters (priests) do not term guilt and sin to be disadvantages foreseeing loss of virtue rather they derive thrill, pleasure and joy of having added an advantage to what would have been a permanent damage to the conscience and ego of the man. Male privilege, for that matter, is conducted to profit motives or surplus material gifts. The question arises as to how and why one can approve formation of absolutely selfish pursuits deferring a commitment for holiness and sanctity? It is to be seen that individual himself develops an impersonal form that sustains in him a regality of fractional and fictional emotions; consequently what happens is separation of will from emotions, idea from attitude and truth from reality. It means that individual goes for a change through those terms and conditions which he himself never approves. Disapproval of an immediate form applies wrong terms of applicability. For example, in the above utterance, object and subject enhance diversion of attitude for promoting the assertion through deviant perception and by closing option for immediate strength. Two priests and a girl, on this occasion, are determined to control the intensity of presentation. Effective methods are inaugurated to compensate the degeneration of an attitude. The first priest, and, later the second priest, becomes convenient to the excellence of illusion whose immediate object is lust. There cannot be any denying of the fact that temporary attitudinal strength entails the loss of existence either in the form of demolished subject or improvised object. The crucial problem that is being faced by priest(s) and the girl is that they are conditionally and situationally not in a position to extend themselves, hence, each is contributing to have an excess through unconvincing margins of the instincts. The first priest is sinful in having claimed unreasonable favour for him by upholding the merit of lust, and the second priest suffers in consequence of that. For this reason, the primacy of reduction is to be seen, found, heard and located in the first only. The decline of truth is an obvious annihilation on the part of the first priest and supposedly unexpected intervention into this received intention by the first renders the situation to be very complex and difficult. The girl, who loses traditional form and privacy, is temporary mark of something that lies between truth and falsehood. Her motive is not wrong yet her approach to constituting an opposition to the advances of the priest is not thoroughly well defined. She lacks a structure for courage that promotes strength, and therefore, she does not compose consciousness for sufficiently realizing wrong terms hence inexplicable odds are working against her. In this situation, the scope of conjunction is in the form of inharmonious object, and is also apparently the framework. The beginning of narrative on a note of disappointment is itself a proof of the fact that there is a continuous subtraction of conceptual paradigms hence the first priest prolonged in sin and lust (not in virtue and goodness) through the second priest, who unconsciously supported in the pursuit of degeneration by the girl who stands in between these two agents of decay. It would mean that the equative form would obtain description in the following manner:

$$A = A - B$$

$$B = B - C$$

$$C = A - B$$

(*A*, *B* and *C* being the first priest, the second priest and the girl respectively.) This is a rather simple process in which an individual comes to the determination through prospective decrease in relative conviction and other formal orientation(s) of the attitude. The function that is presented to characters is dislocated through an interactive alliance inasmuch as each of these is truthfully in a position to acknowledge what each of these is not, and, in that context, appearance is equal to reality and multiplies itself and generates illusion, therefore, reality is also illusion. This groundwork would suggest that intersection of different actions on a factual object not always terminated in a determinate form and determinate prospect. For that matter, indetermination of reality is one of the complications occasioned by the narrative, we are considering. Elsewhere, in *The Decameron*, the narrative situation is rather compulsive in nature. For example, look at the following from the narrative that appears on the fifth day:

> "Keep thy distance", Cimon, "in God's name"
>
> Whereto Cimon made an answer:
>
> "I will come with thee"
>
> 'Tis now for me to show thee, O! Iphegenia how great is my love for thee, that I am grown a man, no doubt it I shall have thee that I shall wax more glorious than a god, a verily thee will I have or die.

In this instance, we understand that the characters (Cimon and Iphegenia) are indefinitely disposed for the sake of immature, inconclusive and incoherent alliance with material body in which either of the characters does not have any truth as such. Cimon is enraged, therefore, he is blatant, and does not come up to the promotion of either an idea or knowledge or truth, on the other hand, Iphegenia, accordingly, allows herself to be a fair partner in the decay of truth, knowledge and ideas hence decay becomes a primary principal to obtain a new variation for personality. In equative form, the conjunction shall have a formulation in the following terms:

> 'Twas not at random, as many women do, that I loved Guiscardo; but by deliberate choice I preferred him before all other men, and of determinate forethought I lured him to my love, whereof, through his and my discretion and constancy, I have long had joyance. Wherein 'twould seem that thou, following rather the opinion of the vulgar than the dictates of truth, find cause to childe me more severely than in my sinful love, for, as if thou wouldst not have been vexed, had my choice fallen on a nobleman, thou complainest that I have foregathered with a man of low condition; and dost not see that therein thou censurest not my fault but that of Fortune, which not seldom raises the unworthy to high place and leaves the worthiest in low estate.
>
> – Boccaccio 1951: 270

Here appearance of an individual finds an application in reciprocal disappearance in the cumulative situation hence it is open to inquiry if the purpose of presentation through a systematic chain of pursuits is to create an authentic standard/ form/character and beyond this, does an individual find himself in a position to raise, ennoble or elevate? Parallel reading of the situation from the side of the character as well as individual derives an idea that an action comes as an effect of wonder to the individual/character to explicate correlated attitudes of surprise and amazement. To compensate this, an individual/ object proceeds to abruptly respond to the situation without any necessary preparation on his part, consequently, he throws open for himself a host of misplaced notion. Even in John Bunyan's *The Pilgrim's Progress*, the entire situation is fairly close to this, look at the following, for example:

> Atheist: "I laugh to see what ignorant persons you are, to take upon you so tedious a journey; and yet are like to have nothing but your travel for your pains."
>
> Christian: "Why, man? Do you think we shall not be received?"

> Atheist: "Received! There is no such place as you dream of in all this world."
>
> Christian: "But there is in the world to come."
>
> Atheist: "When I was at home in mine own country, I heard as you now affirm, and from that hearing went out to see, and have been seeking this city this twenty years. But find no more of it than I did the first day I set out."
>
> Christian: "We have both heard and believed that there is such a place to be found."
>
> Atheist: "Had not I, when at home, believed, I had not come thus far to seek. But finding none (and yet I should, had there been such a place to be found, for I have gone to seek it further than you), I am going back again, and will seek to refresh myself with the things that I then cast away, for hopes of that which, I now see, is not."
> – Bunyan 1969: 124

Here in this place, conjunction becomes a mode of negotiation settled through persuasion, submission, contempt and even subjugation. The inquisitive model allows the presentation of curiosity and wonder in terms of established truth hence the object and the subject (Christian/Atheist) involved in the process are as indeterminate and inauthentic as any illusion or temptation, for that matter, may be. Christian, in the present context, locates an object (reception at the gate of Heaven) yet structure of the object is vague and infinite. In illustrating this curiosity to the strength of truth, Christian discourages himself and is brought nearer to something (Atheist) in whom the reality is only an abstraction hence his approach precisely becomes an aberration in experience about which we cannot have any ideational formulation, consequently, Atheist has an opportunity to demolish the conduct of right model (wisdom, virtue, grace and fortitude) inasmuch as he finds an illusion (getting Christian deviated) and reconstructs a temptation (revival of material form in Christian). It is now obviously a deformation of extended personality and brought to a level-playing field. Extension of Christian is basically not at all an extension of his strength rather it is curious imbalance that is disengaging himself.

He is only successful in manifesting an inverted form for him rather than soliciting eternal meaning inherent upon the situation. On the other hand, the Atheist, by motivating the consciousness, finds an opportunity to prepare a model of conjunction by inviting Christian to demolish conviction, persuasion, inheritance and embodiment hence nearly every form of permanent ethos. There is a series of interplay and interposition, which develop a commitment. In Christian, ability to develop curious persuasion is rather limited and immature, yet he is a seeker in the path of knowledge while atheist embodies an authority through imposition, and he continues to render himself absolute until and unless a higher form appears to demolish the sanctity of his authority. The nature of time communicates an act of attitude or temperament. The first important characteristic of such conjunctive interplay would be the willingness to face the rapidity of transformation, which, in turn, would be internal or external. In internally assorted change, the subject and the object are in a position to open up their primary structure and content so as to make out a complete identification of one with the another while external changes are distinctly imposed either by the subject on the object or by the object on the subject. In the present situation, Atheist has an upper hand. He obtains associative conjunction in such a way that position of the content is temporarily displaced, and such a regressive structure conceives formative principle underlying the necessity of growing and acting to the completion and conclusion when a logical aberration brings forth a crisis in inception of reality, the method of creating an attitude for the sake of rounded activities becomes less and less. To view the manner of conduct, individuality decays and renders each other decadent by sheer powers of absorption. Expressive categories in Atheist (excess of wrath and excess of jealousy) nearly approve corresponding credentials of goodness and decency. In Christian, for example, in the following, we have a fairer chance to see how compulsive he is at work:

> Christian: "Why, man? Do you think we shall not be received?"
>
> Atheist: "Received! There is no such place as you dream of in all this world." – Bunyan 1969: 124

Christian elevates himself, and, for that matter, he seems to be conforming to collective paradigm of purity, truth, privilege and honour, and circumstantially commits himself to genuine concept for each of these. For example, goodness in him is an innate nature and a property for refinement of object/subject/form, yet this procedure of change for the sake of any privilege in Atheist is almost impossible. Atheist consumes nobler content and therefore disallows himself to be reasonably oriented towards truth. The way in which John Bunyan has maintained the viability of opposition though mutation is remarkable in the circumstances in the foregoing. Here deviation caused by Atheist appears always in regression, and never in progression. For this reason, he moves from primordial beginning and takes narrative to the scale of curiosity and wonder.

The scale for conjunction is a matter of contextual adequacy or inadequacy, and accordingly, conjunction could either be appropriate or inappropriate to the relevancy or irrelevancy. In the tales of King Arthur methodically irregular conjunctions appear to sustain the logic of generation (falling union, warmth, experience, imagination) and the like. King Arthur himself is borne out of an irregular, abstract genitive conformity. Lust of a lady primarily invokes attitudinal fallacies and to sanction this crisis male appears. In an event such as this, function of form in to propose an end to conformity and involvement. Life does not authenticate either the external intensity or depth in being able to form a continuity of appearance. The appearance becomes an illusion of perception and romance is wanting in the adequacy of substance and figures of reception. The purpose of approaching an interface with the optimum condition obtained in either object or subject is a primary elevation for the situation. Appearance always enters into the functioning of conduct and reception, therefore, the question does not simply arise if the progression of resultant variable is obtained through addition or multiplication to situate a unit if individual's conscience in the supplementary existence of some individuals would be an exercise to be preferred for the sake of largeness and strength of the situation. Sometimes a crisis is felt in disposing those objects which constitute relation amongst themselves, and on that account, undivided/objects/forms in narrative for an exclusion from the interrelated proposition. The worth of remark could be completely realized in the following episodes from Pāli Jātakas:

> अतीते वाराणस्यां ब्रह्मदत्ते राज्यं कुर्वति हिमवत् प्रदेशे बोधिसत्त्वः कपिन्योनां निर्वृत्य नागबलः स्थामसम्पन्नो महाशरीरः सौभाग्यप्राप्तो भूत्वा गगनिवर्तने अरण्यामतने वासमचिल्कित् । तदा गग्यामेकः शिशुमारोऽवात्सीत् । अथाऽत्य भार्या बोधिसत्त्वस्य शरीरं दृष्ट्वा तस्य हृदयमांसे दोहदमुत्पाद्य शिशुमारमाह – 'अहं स्वामिन! एतस्य कपिराजस्य हृदयमांसं खादितुकामा' इति । 'भद्रे! वयं जलगोचराः, एष स्थलगोचरः, किमिनि तं ग्रहीतुं शक्ष्यामः' इति । 'येन केनोपायेन गृहाण, चेन्न लप्स्य मरिष्यामि' इति 'तेन मा भैषीः, अस्त्येक उपायः इति खादयिश्यामि त्वां तस्य हृदयमांसम्' इति । शिशुमारीं समाश्वास्य बोधिसत्त्वस्य गगयाः पानीयं पीत्वां गगतीरे । निषण्णकाले अन्तिकं गत्वा एवमाह वानरेन्द्र । अस्मिन प्रदेशे कष्टफलानि खादन् कि त्वं चीणैस्थान एव चरसि । पारगगयां आम्रलकुचादीनां मधुफलानां अन्तो नास्ति, किं त तत्र गत्वा फलाफलं खादितुं न वर्तते इति । 'कुम्भीलराज! गंग महोदका विस्तीर्णा, कथं तत्र गमिष्यामि' इति । 'चेत् गच्छसि अहं त्वां मम पृष्ठमारोप्य नेष्यामि' इति ।
>
> *atīte vārāṇasyāṁ brahmadatte rājyaṁ kurvati himavat pradeśe bodhisattvaḥ kapinyonāṁ nirvṛtya nāgabalaḥ sthāmasampanno mahāśarīraḥ saubhāgyaprāpto bhūtvā gaganivartane araṇyāmatane vāsamacilkit* । *tadā gagyāmekaḥ śiśumāro 'vātsīt* । *athā 'tya bhāryā bodhisattvasya śarīraṁ dṛṣṭvā tasya hṛdayamāṁse dohadamutpādya śisumāramāha – 'ahaṁ svāmin! etasya kapirājasya hṛdayamāṁsaṁ khāditukāmā' iti* । *'bhadre! vayaṁ jalagocarāḥ, eṣa sthalagocaraḥ kimini taṁ grahītuṁ śakṣyāmaḥ' iti* । *'yena kenopāyena gṛhāṇa, cenna lapsya mariṣyāmi' iti 'tena mā bhaiṣīḥ, astyeka upāyaḥ iti khādayiśyāmi tvāṁ tasya hṛdayamāṁsam' iti* । *śiśumārīṁ samāśvāsya bodhisattvasya gagayāḥ pānīyaṁ pītvāṁ gagatīre* । *niṣaṇṇakāle antikaṁ gatvā evamāha vānarendra* । *asmin pradeśe kaṣṭaphalāni khādan ki tvaṁ cīṇaisthāna eva carasi* । *pāragagayāṁ āmralakucādīnāṁ madhuphalānāṁ anto nāsti, kiṁ ta tatra gatvā phalāphalaṁ khādituṁ na vartate iti* । *'kumbhīlarāja! gaṅga mahodakā vistīrṇā, kathaṁ tatra gamiṣyāmi' iti* । *'cet gacchasi ahaṁ tvāṁ mama pṛṣṭhamāropya neṣyāmi' iti* ।
>
> – *Pālijātakāvalyām, Śiśumārajātakam*, p. 1

In this situation, the scope of conjunction is large and wide.

The strength of situation comes from extreme idealization of characters and the action grows to such an extent that immensity of wonder and surprise becomes logically coincidental with the whole situation. The Monkey and Crocodile on the one hand, and wife to Crocodile on the other, develop a scale for conjunction. Monkey is a natural formation of both the inquisitions curiously mounted on wonder and the power, who displays his excellence in obtaining a term for regression of Crocodile and his wife. Crocodile, at the beginning, possesses effective strength of false wisdom, false insight and the like to convince equals with the power of regressive terms and forms. There can be no success in deducting logically inconclusive terms and because of this he could only encourage and excite and demolish the fragmentary events in him. His appearance is unsuitable to the development of an action of compromise on equal conditions. To deal with the situation, the Monkey shows an opening through a better enlargement of his attitude, ideas and convictions. In this action, the beginning is in the manner of addition where ego meets ego and conscience meets conscience, for this reason, both Monkey and Crocodile could stand to the growth of individual authority. Unfortunately, the authority in Crocodile is disgraced and becomes secondary to thought and perception. Meaning of this action could be said to have opened to determination through resolution and irresolution. Monkey's perception could frankly explicate a culmination of imminence and immaterial and inauthentic compulsion and inquisition primarily to constitute purer model of truth. Monkey's growth through a natural inquisition does indeed verify the problem of non-ego being in the hand of Crocodile in such a difficult merger of attitudes. There can be no definite resolvable situation rather expansion of a method in a situation is explicated via inconsequential show of excess authority. It would be better to say that the Monkey as a character adds to himself, for this reason, his resultant is variously situated in the manner of enlargement of truth. In equative measure, the situation could be held to be adhering to the following form:

$$A = A^{+} = A^{n}.$$

Here *A* is Monkey himself whose extension is felt beyond addition and till infinity. This embodiment in characteral formation concludes opposition with regard to a controlled flow of truthful uniformity and thoughtful excellence. In respect of Crocodile the process of merger into an extended form is stopped and marked with humiliation and contempt. Precise reason is not that he is unconsciously or consciously a privileged destroyer of authentic virtue rather it lies in wrong creation of additive measure when only subtraction could have been the meaning (to be able to disclose the intention midway where only patience and quiet would have been the better option). The focus on relative insufficiency of attitude formation results in Crocodile being relegated to an awkward and generally disgraceful environment. The following utterance of Crocodile's spouse would make the point clearer:

> अहं स्वामिन्! एतस्य कपिराजस्य हृदयमांसं खादितुकामा ।
>
> *ahaṁ svāmin! etasya kapirājasya hṛdayamāṁsaṁ khāditukāmā* ।
>
> – *Pālijātakāvalyām*, *Śiśumārajātakam*, p. 1

We can understand that the position of Crocodile's spouse is not equal to the truth that is looming large on the occasion, that is why desire to have the Monkey as a food generally imbalances the situation. Urgency through a motivation is not something that could be mentioned in ethical or moral terms of addition.

The movement of conjunction (primarily addition and multiplication) in the above situation displaces content of truth nevertheless it is restored for the sake of goodness. The question of forming a progression for the sake of benefit of both compulsive and ennobled forms in a given narrative situation speaks of process of enlargement of content and form. In *The Pilgrim's Progress*, the application of a utility and significance is worth the attention:

> So when the morning was come, the giant goes to them again, and takes them into the castle-yard, and shows them, as his wife had bidden him. "These", said he, "were pilgrims as you are, once, and they trespassed in my grounds, as you have done; and when I thought fit, I tore them in pieces; and so within ten days

> I will do you. Go get you down to your den again." And with that he beat them all the way thither.
>
> "What a fool," quoth he, "am I, thus to lie in a stinking durgeon when I may as well walk at liberty? I have a key in my bosom, called Promise, that will (I am persuaded) open any lock in Doubting Castle. Then said Hopeful, "That's good news; good brother pluck it out of thy bosom and try." – Bunyan 1969: 109

Here compulsive form initiates methodical recognition through mutual interjection. In each such interjection we cannot see a stretch of denial through inverted orientation. The giant does not conduct nor does he recruit a term for association. He commands a will for an advancement of threat purporting/presupposing/envisaging inhibitions that nowhere negotiate adjustment. Giant generates and enacts prohibitory contents unusual and extraordinary compulsive forms. The form of the character is open for perpetual disappearance from normative groundwork. Each utterance stores up normative material in whose models, forms/characters realize illusion. This is to say that characters do not undergo any referential derangement as such at the behest of seeming probability or improbability. The question arises as to how and why characters at work become conditionally inoperative and undergo figural aberration? The answer to the question must be sought in pragmatic disorder and irrational systematization which are at the heart of Western thinking process. Western mode of thinking absolutely excludes comprehensible cognition therefore apprehension is motivated to relocate near total fragmentation of knowledge.

In the above situation, the object and the subject (Giant/Christian) are ironically displaced from one another in a manner in which there is no common idea to have parallel growth. Giant is excessively responsive hence he always rounds off contents whereas Christian, even while he stands for the sake of truth, is deprived of the benefit of terms. The change of laws of addition for the sake of Giant and degradation of contents for Christian are not to be justified through wilful forms and purposes. It stops the evolution and places contents through explanatory obstacle for that matter appropriate objects which are so unable to describe the figure of truth and knowledge in the present case. As a matter of fact action intended to be conducted by the Giant becomes inoperative and inactive leading to aberration and error. This has a serious effect on Christian who performs a radical dissolution of the notion of abstraction yet he (Christian) does not have success as such in obtaining the truth. He becomes defunct and discredits the choice presented to him by the strength underlying the events. It can be seen that resolution is deferred and conjunctions become independent of one another.

The reliability of assertion in the form of conjunction is greatly affected by position and centrality of character/individual/form/objects inasmuch as option for negotiation immediately changes or alters the sanctity of action and resolves it into conscious equivalents. It happens in such a way that model for association are openly and convincingly subscribed to a concrete perception enjoyed by a form/character and there is nothing that would turn it into rigidity and inflexibility of the materials constituting an action. For example, in the following narrative episode, position occupied by the character Bhairava tells us how stretch of a form could enliven generosity of ethos although in the present circumstance, generous disposition leads to catastrophe and disaster yet it recognizes the principle and method one could adopt in looking at the characters:

आसीत्कल्याणकटकवास्तव्यो भैरवो नाम व्याधः । स चैकदा मृगमन्विष्यमाणो विन्ध्याटवीं गतवान् । ततस्तेन व्यापादितं मृगमादाय गच्छता घोराकृतिः शूकरो दृष्टः । तेन व्याधेन मृगं भूमौ निधाय शूकरः शरेणाहतः । शूकरेणापि घनघोरगर्जनं कृत्वा स व्याधो मुष्कदेशे हतः संश्छिन्नाद्रुम इव भूमौ निपपात ।

अथ तयोः पादास्फालनेन सर्पोऽपि मृतः । अथानन्तरं दीर्घरावो नाम जम्बुकः परिभ्रमन्नाहारार्थी तान्मृतान्मृगव्याधसर्पशूकरान पश्यत् । अचिन्तयभा – 'अहो! अद्य महरोज्यं मे समुपस्थितम् ।

ततः प्रथमबुभुक्षायामिदं निःस्वादु कोदण्डलग्नं स्नायुबन्धनं खादामि ।' इत्युक्त्वा तथा कृते सति छिन्नो स्नायुबन्धनं उत्पतितेन धनुषा हृदि निर्भिन्नाः स दीर्घरावः पत्वं गतः । अतोऽहं ब्रवीमि – "कर्तव्यः संचयो नित्यम्" इत्यादि ।

*āsītkalyāṇakaṭakavāstavyo bhairavo nāma vyādhaḥ* | *sa caikadā mṛgamanviṣyamāṇo vindhyāṭavīṁ gatavān* | *tatastena vyāpāditaṁ mṛgamādāya gacchatā ghorākṛtiḥ śūkaro dṛṣṭaḥ* । *tena vyādhena mṛgaṁ bhūmau nidhāya śūkaraḥ śareṇāhataḥ* । *śūkareṇāpi ghanaghoragarjanaṁ kṛtvā sa vyādho muṣkadeśe hataḥ saṁśchisrādruma iva bhūmau nipapāta* ।

*atha tayoḥ pādāsphālanena sarpo 'pi mṛtaḥ* । *athāntaraṁ dīrgharāvo nāma jambukaḥ paribhramasrāhārārthī tānmṛtānmṛgavyādhasarpaśūkarā na paśyat* । *acintayabhā – 'aho! adya maharojyaṁ me samupasthitam* ।

*tataḥ prathamabubhukṣāyāmidaṁ niḥsvādu kodaṇḍalagnaṁ snāyubandhanaṁ khādāmi* ।*' ityuktvā tathā kṛte sati chisro snāyubandhanaṁ utpatitena dhanuṣā hadi nirbhisrāḥ sa dīrgharāvaḥ patvaṁ gataḥ* । *ato 'haṁ bravīmi – "kartavyaṁ sañcayo nityam" ityādi* ।

– *Hitopadeśa*, pp. 63-64

The culmination of all the active contents of action into one grand whole is a feature of conjunction that is to be recognized. Bhairava initiates the action and the Pig (*śūkara*) carries the action forward, and the Deer (*mṛga*) and the Snake (*sarpa*) are passive attendants on the situation while Jackal (*dīrgharāva*) is a correlative standing between the Snake and Bhairava. It means that Bhairava not only begets the action but also embodies keenness and thirst for receiving unknown form of benefit/loss sanctioned to an enraged spirit. This conduct is quite suitable to the urgency of situation yet strong opposition in resolving the meaningful term presented by the Pig is equal to the resolve of Bhairava, therefore, both of them have no option but to succumb to death. This is not a final resolution rather three allied parties in this scheme of multiplication of calculative or relative death in the form of *mṛga*, *sarpa* and *dīrgharāva*. The strength of expression is equal to the power of action unfolded in universal correlatives obtained within it and schematically it is concretized in the following rationale:

$$A = A^{+} A^{+} \rightarrow A^{++} = A^{n} + A.$$

It can be understood that beginning and end of conjunction are obtained in the absolute form of Bhairava. To understand a situation like that, one must focus the attention on the direction of concern and transfer of an attitude to create models for perception, and in this context rage of Bhairava is primarily correlated by multiplication of further intensities in rage and ferocity, and in that way completes the process of destruction of each and every body.

It shows quite clearly that the Deer could not have been dead had Bhairava not initiated the action, and, in turn, *śūkara* must not have died had the Deer not been killed and Snake would not have been otherwise dead had Bhairava, *mṛga*, *śukara* and *sarpa* would not have been deceiving one another in that the formulation of an equation of this strength would draw upon a necessity of proving the point that beginning through an end is always beginning of course through an intervention of rising situation leading to association and falling situation leading to dissociation. There can be no doubt as to what fostered the intensity of extraordinary wonder and curiosity brought about in internal creation of Bhairava in the form of one who directs primary of action towards complete indivisibility is remarkable and we can only wonder the fact that his chief instrument in the progress of an action is also mounted on the scale of enrichment and refinement and universality. The situation is really a pragmatic extension of high resolution conceived in absolute form hence it must have the attendance of correlative figures though a developing system of perceptible sequence is like following:

$$A = A^{+} + A^{++} + A^{(n+n)}.$$

In this, $A$ would be determinate absolute of Bhairava and his variants in the form of *mṛga* and *jambūka* have their formation in the continuity of surplus situation like $A^{+}$ $A^{++}$ but each, in turn, returns to the nativity of initiation in Bhairava himself. It also leads to suffering and strengthening of constituents of truth and assertion. Bhairava proceeds with commitment and comes to terms with material form of commitment, for that matter, killing of the animals is not at all a sign of loss for him but is a situation of strength and virtue for him. In other words he (Bhairava) continues to enact formative negotiation for synthesizing the random factors in minor attendants to the situation (*mṛga*, *sarpa*, *śūkara*, *jambūka*) distributed unevenly in whole environment. It is only he who picks up each of them and brings them closer and together in such a way that a synthesis could be brought about.

Bhairava assumes a rather insignificant position in establishing a direct route to invent an unnatural form of his virtues, or for that matter, assigns a worthy place to each and everybody tentatively. This idea could assume empirical form if Bhairava could be stated to be as destroyer and inventor of term and condition of the life of animals who have come face to face with him. Complication that is involved in the case would make us say that Bhairava receives a superimposition of the contents and to each content he gives a new form by maintaining and upholding strength in it.

## VI

Structure of conjunction has a method for revival and regeneration of any category of human conception. For example, it can revive and regenerate the motives of thought, experience, and language in which the primary situation of evocation by addition leads to an emergence of necessity to an adjunct of form through modified sensibility and attendant perception. In *The Canterbury Tales*, we can understand the strength of narrative:

*Whan that Arcite to Thebes comen was,*
*Ful ofte a day he swelte and seyde 'allas,'*
*For seen his lady shal he never-mo.*
*And shortly to concluden al his wo,*
*So muche sorwe had never creature*
*That is, or shal, whyl that world may dure.*
*His sleep, his mete, his drink in him biraft,*
*That lene he wex, and drye as is a shaft.*
*His eyen holwe, and grisly to biholde;*
*And Solitarie he was, and ever alone,*
*And wailling al the night, making his mone.*
*And if he herde song or instrument,*
*Then wolde he wepe, he mighte not be stent;*
*So feble eek were his spirits, and so lowe,*
*And Chaunged so, that no man coude knowe*
*His Speche nor his vois, though men it herde.*
*And in his gere, for al the world he ferde*

*Nat oonly lyk the lovers Maladye*
*Of Heroes, but rather lyk manye*
*Engendred of humour malencolyk,*
*Biforen, in his celle fantastyk.*
*And shortly, turned was al up-so-doun*
*Bothe habit and eek disposicioun*
*Of him, this woful lovere daun Arcite.*
– Chaucer 1958: 40

In this narrative account, Geoffrey Chaucer projects the subject as if the subject is in the process of reinvention, and continuity of reception is assorted in irregular formation of experiential motive. Arcite is a character in whom the purpose of conceiving a direct presentation to the object or the subject lies in making himself idealized through an exploration of similar attitude in different objects. In this situation, Arcite suffers because love hasn't brought about fulfilment to him, rather it has dissociated him from concern of beloved. This proves the point that emergence from this situation has found and obtained in him a private orientation towards the subject. Arcite has to enact himself through recently enriched and renewed presentation of experience and perception and both of these are simultaneously motivated for the sake of attendance in truthful form. Chaucer's style in rendering the terms normal certainly appears to be a method in expounding a concept of conjunction. Here Arcite is the primary centre of extension of general ethos involved in the expression of love and exposition of love through a composition of realized experience. Arcite connects him to the external space and, in the first place, introduces the character of objects and in each he could transform himself. This ensures the manner of extension and enlargement in so far as individual himself is proclaiming himself listening and himself disembodying the whole statement, yet externals of universal space provide him with a background and foreground to the situation, surprisingly, in each, there is a rise of Arcite as a character. The process through which Arcite is left to supplement a richer and wider variation in his own personality is perhaps one of the central factors in marking out his projection. It is also to be understood that Arcite is criss-crossed between appearance and reality without knowing that magnitude of time and factors of space are, at once, in high imminence. Growth of narrative and action intended in Arcite opts for a total inclusion hence event (love) and object (Arcite) constantly merge into each other. The beginning is made in a fair assessment of primary terms and the benefits that time could pass on to necessity of action, therefore, the character is introduced through repulsive motion where neither the object nor the subject could attract each other. In this circumstance, Chaucer through Arcite develops situational urgency that culminates in separation (of Arcite from Emily) through acute theatrical terms. The adequacy of context in synthesizing conjunction appears to be slightly overworked inasmuch as approved formation and tertiary inceptions are relatively not so much interacted in deviating logical and normal grounds of cohesion. To build a construction across a solid ground would be to expound a series of firmer structures hence in narratives the development of characters into forms of conjunction is very important. If a character could conceive primary forms right at the beginning he will have an opportunity to devise correlatives for his wisdom. For example, look at the formation, outlining a generous system of terms of association:

अस्ति यौवनश्रीनगरे मन्दमतिर्नाम रथकार: । स च स्वभार्यां बन्धकीं जानाति । जारेण समं स्वचक्षुषा नैकस्थाने पश्यति । ततोऽसौ रथकार: 'अहमन्यं ग्रामं गच्छामि' इत्युक्त्वा चलित: । कियद्दूरं गत्वा पुनरागत्य पर्यटतले स्वगृहे निभृतं स्थित: । अथ 'रथकारो ग्रामान्तरं गत:' इत्युपजातविमस: स जार: संध्याकाल एवागत: । पचात्तेत समं तस्मिन्पर्यटे क्रीडन्ती पर्यटतलस्थितस्य भर्तु: किंचिदग्स्पर्शात्स्वामिनं मायाविनमिति विज्ञाय विषण्णाऽभवत् । ततो जारेणोक्तम् – 'किमिति त्वमद्य मया सह निर्भरं न रमसे? विस्मितेव प्रतिभासि मे त्वम्'। तयोक्तम् – 'अनभिज्ञोऽसि। मम प्राणेम्रो येन ममाकौमारं सख्यं सोऽद्य ग्रामान्तरं गत: । तेन विना सकलजनपूर्णोऽपि ग्रामो मां प्रत्यरण्यवरति । 'किं भावि, तत्र परस्थाने, किं खादितवान्, कथं वा प्रसुप्त:' इत्यस्मद्घ्रदयं विदीर्यते ।' जारो ब्रूते – 'तब किमेवं स्नेहभूमी रथकार:? बन्धक्यवदत् – 'रे बर्बर् ! किं वदसि?

त्वं जार: पापमति: । मनोलौल्यात्पुष्पताम्बूलसदृश: कदाचित्स्येव्यसे कदाचिस्त्रा सेव्यसे च । स च स्वामी मां विक्रेतुं देवेभ्यो ब्राह्मणेभ्योऽपि दातुमीम्र: । किं बहुना, तस्मिजीवति जीवामि, तन्मरणे चानुमरणं करिष्यामीति प्रतिज्ञा वर्तते ।

*asti yauvanaśrīnagare mandamatirnāma rathakāraḥ* । *sa ca svabhāryāṁ bandhakīṁ jānāti* । *jāreṇa samaṁ svacakṣuṣā naikasthāne paśyati* । *tato 'sau rathakāraḥ 'ahamanyaṁ grāmaṁ gacchāmi' ityuktvā calitaḥ* । *kiyaddūraṁ gatvā punarāgatya paryaṭatale svagṛhe nibhṛtaṁ sthitaḥ* । *atha 'rathakāro grāmāntaraṁ gataḥ' ityupajātavimasaḥ sa jāraḥ sandhyākāla evāgataḥ* । *pacātteta samaṁ tasminparyaṭe krīḍantī paryaṭatalasthitasya bhartuḥ kiñcidagsparśātsvāminaṁ māyāvinamiti vijñāya viṣaṇṇā 'bhavat* । *tato jāreṇoktam – 'kimiti tvamadya mayā sena nirbharaṁ na ramase? vismiteva pratibhāsi me tvam'* । *tayoktam – 'anabhijño 'si* । *mama prāṇemro yena mamākaumāraṁ sakhyaṁ so 'dya grāmāntaraṁ gataḥ* । *tena vinā sakalajanapūrṇo 'pi grāmo māṁ pratyaraṇyavarati* । *'kiṁ bhāvi, tatra parasthāne, kiṁ khāditavān, kathaṁ vā prasuptaḥ' ityasmadbradayaṁ vidīryate* ।*' jaro brūte – 'taba kimevaṁ snehabhūmī rathakāraḥ? bandhakyavadat – 're barbar! kiṁ vadasi?*

*tvaṁ jāraḥ pāpamatiḥ* । *manolaulyātpuṣpatāmbūlasadṛśaḥ kadācitsyevyase kadācisrā sevyase ca* । *sa ca svāmī māṁ vikretuṁ devebhyo brāhmaṇebhyo 'pi dātumīmraḥ* । *kiṁ bahunā, tasmijīvati jīvāmi, tanmaraṇe cānumaraṇaṁ kariṣyāmīti pratijñā vartate* ।

– *Hitopadeśa*, p. 169

There is a purpose in presenting a structure of reality through inadvertent explication of truth. The author creates three dimension(s) – truth, reality and illusion – with such a precision that each form has a full-length assertion. Truth is a sign of proclamation to associate a condition of virtue necessitated by a range of assertion and exclamation. The necessity of content in situation is developed through a mature process of participation. For a character, supposition is not even a fragment of visual reality. It inhabits those necessary functions of truth which acquire maturity in hard and strong reasons. In the context, we can understand that Bandhakī merits a purpose in effecting truth/ illusion by creating varieties of appearance. In each appearance, Bhandhakī participates with grace, honour and conviction. Her attitude is open to submission and for a submission she revives both purpose and craving in the falsehood. Truth is not what is claimed to be the procedure rather it is an association of an illusion with conviction in such a way that both are mutually adaptable. Bandhakī applies the value of illusory figure on the current action so as to enact a deviance in the perception. The strength of perception is enhanced through the modification of logic of generation contained in configurable object and perceptible subject, and the reason obtained in consequence of random motion, individual temperament and attitude. On the other hand, the subject's affirmation of attitude is realized in appropriate accent, right comprehension of the falling situation, and for this purpose, Bandhakī has an upper hand.

In this narration, the strength of conviction multiplies the agents of harmony and therefore Bandhakī is in a position to revive her in the situation. On the other hand, Rathakāra and Jāra both are fragmentary and reversible formation because of the reason that Rathakāra does not explicate conviction from truth and reason, from sensation, and subsequently, he disqualifies both fact and reason in being demotivated and destructive. Here ideational inconsistency of Rathakāra is something that is to be taken to the notice and one must find that his ideals are really incapable of extracting the figures as normal choices in the ordinary circumstances hence culminates in a natural rejection in the hands of compulsive.

## VII

There is a purpose in presenting the view of reality through inadvertent explication of truth. The author creates three dimensions: – truth, reality and illusion – with a provision that each form has a full-length assertion. Truth is a sign of proclamation to associate a condition of virtue with a form of assessment and evolution. The necessity of presuming worth of content in situation is developed through a mature process of participation for a character in which supposition is not even a fragment of visual reality. It inhabits those necessary functions of truth which acquire maturity in hard and strong reason. In the content we can understand that Bandhakī merits a purpose in effecting truth/illusion by creating varieties of appearance. In each appearance, she participates with grace, honour and dignity. Her attitude is open to submission, and for a submission, she revives both purpose and meaning in falsehood. Truth is not what is claimed to be the product of reality, rather it is an association of an illusion and conviction in such a way that both are mutually adaptable. Bandhakī applies the value of illusory figure on the current action so as to enact a deviance in the perception. The strength of perception is enhancing through the modification of the logic in the object and the subject. Object reasons are confirmed to random individual temperament and attitudes. On the other hand, in subject affirmation to attitude is realized with upcoming accent and right presentation of the falling situation and to this purpose Bandhakī has an upper hand.

In this narrative, the strength of conviction multiplies the agents of harmony and, therefore, lady Bandhakī is in a position to revive her in the situation. On the other hand, Rathakāra and Jāra both are fragmentary and reversible formations because of the reason that Rathakāra does not explicate the conviction from the truth and reason from the sensation, and subsequently, he disqualifies both the fact and reason of being demotivated and destructive. In this situation, the ideational inconsistency of Rathakāra is something to be taken to the notice and one must find that his ideals are really incapable of extracting the figure as the normal choice of an individual in the ordinary circumstances. This culminates into a natural rejection in the hands of experience and compulsive form. He commits a mistake in granting an authority of sensation to someone in compliance with his demotivation from the models of truth and purity. The position of Jāra (a friend of Bandhakī) is also not quite sound. He has entered into an alliance with Bandhakī in which there is only access of sensory models, hence his presentations are not wholly incongruous but indecorous as well. He cannot construct a position of permanence with regard to motivation and therefore he is demolished simply because of the fact that external variants (especially sensory embodiment) do not enter into his exhortations to revive himself. He demotivates the purpose by recognizing a situational term to be the permanent fabric of the body of truth. Looking at the treachery and fraud on experience and conscience, we can understand that amongst Bandhakī, Rathakāra and Jāra, it is only Bandhakī who opts for a natural and significant retention of herself, and, in that way, obtains better conjunction. In having been touched by the husband beneath the bed the utterance of Bandhakī is remarkable:

> ततो जारेणोक्तम् - 'किमिति त्वमद्य मया सह निर्भरं न रमसे? विस्मितेव प्रतिभासि मे त्वम्'। तयोक्तम् - 'अनभिज्ञोऽसि । मम प्राणेम्रो येन ममाकौमारं सख्यं सोऽद्य ग्रामान्तरं गतः ।'
>
> *tato jāreṇoktam – 'kimiti tvamadya mayā saha nirbharaṁ na ramase? vismiteva pratibhāsi me tvam' । tayoktam – 'anabhijño 'si । mama prāṇemro yena mamākaumāraṁ sakhyaṁ so 'dya grāmāntaraṁ gataḥ ।'*
>
> – *Hitopadeśa*, p. 169

This is an illustration of the fact that in the time of advancement of sensory application to the rage explicates the truth through illusion, and Bandhakī is exactly performing whole the necessary decencies to revive herself in the situation. Truth, in this action, is an extraordinary intensity of wonder, and, therefore, it is being logically approached through the exterior semblance of the situation. Bandhakī is an arrangement to transform truth into illusory perception and she upholds the merit of deception hidden in unfavourable appearance. Truth is truth so long and so far as equivalent form does not project the sanctity to be false and degenerate, Bandhakī's appearance is to taking advance of this promotional enterprise and, therefore, she says to Jāra:

> . . . अनभिज्ञोऽसि । मम प्राणेम्रो
>
> . . . *anabhijño 'si । mama prāṇemro*
>
> – ibid.

The conduct of characters in explaining the resolution of the crisis (Bandhakī explains to Jāra, Jāra explains to Bandhakī and husband explains to one other than himself), suits to the deviance occasioned by critical nature of perception and expression. Bandhakī stands before Jāra and Rathakāra, standing in between Bandhakī and Jāra, generates a favour from the construction of revival and disappearance caused by them and caused for their own sake.

The idea of rejection of a lady as degraded and as corrupt as Bandhakī could not be the basis of the attitudinal reflection of Rathakāra, rather he goes on to affirm the sanctity and trust and faith and hope in Bandhakī with a renewal of the strength and power. This idea could be comprehended on the basis of fact that primary of goodness is always extraordinary in Indian tradition and no immediate and temporary intervention could demolish the canonical principle. It is in that way; the necessity of conjunction is revived and brought back to the consideration. The instance provided by the urgency of explication does however produce the brilliance of relative maturity of the figures and in a cohesive form the presentation would yield to the following method of division:

| | | |
|---|---|---|
| (Bandhakī) | $A$ | |
| (Rathakāra) | $B$ | $= A$ |
| (Jāra) | $C$ | |

The principle of division necessarily would bring the equality of variants in favour of Bandhakī. In other words, the characteral form would always approximate to an expressive figural option in Bandhakī. The expressive contents sometimes disjoin the internal configuration so as to demarcate the moment of attitude from stationary motive that may be inherent upon the situation. In Thomas Malory's *Le Morte D'Arthur*, we can understand the situation:

> The same night that my lord was dead, the hour of his death, as his Knights record, there came into my castle of Tintagil a man like my lord in speech and in countenance, and two Knights with him in likeness of his two Knights Brastias and Jordanus, and so I went unto bed with him as I ought to do with my lord, and the same night, as I shall answer unto God, this child was begotten upon me. That is truth, said the king, as ye say; for it was I myself that came in the likeness, and therefore dismay yon not, for I am father of the child; and there he told her all the cause, how it was by Merlin's counsel. Then the queen made great joy when she knew who was the father of her child.
>
> – Malory 1996: 4

The basic situation that comes to attend the secondary conception of attitude and ideas is inherent upon usurpation and perception. Perception, in this case, does not project either the knowledge or the idea as being rich and concrete, therefore, it creates subsequent weakness in the character of queen. The queen does not hold the rationality to be an embodiment of truth rather she denounces the concrete forms of truth and enters into an alliance with stranger hence conceives. This proves the point that the categories in her are irrationally created and she expresses the ease in misjudging irrationality so created. She suggests an illusion in such a way that it is not only real but is a coherent model of judgement. The validity of this judgement would be the acceptance of projected model of knowledge rather than conventional and traditional system of value, hence the queen having had a relation with someone other than her husband acquires the position of eminence to make the proclamation of authenticity and authority in the background of the sin, which is further qualified by the birth of Arthur and birth confounds the confusion. This narrative presents three parallel centres of power model so as to develop the contention that ideational intensity is only the strength of deliberate abstraction of the inner contents. Either one can motivate the content or one can demotivate the form of content. In each of the cases the resultant would be the variants in which one form would have been in any relation with the other form and in that way the nature of meaning would be in opposition to the strength that it undertakes to create.

## VIII

The approach of conjunction in the Western narrative is generally projected through concentration and synthesis of imperfect conduction of motives and purposes. For example, look at the following passage:

> The same night that my lord was dead, the hour of his death, as his Knights record, there came into my castle of Tintagil a man like my lord in speech and in countenance, and two Knights Brastias and Jardinus, and so went into bed with him as I ought to do with my lord, and the same night, as I shall answer unto

> God, this child as begotten upon me. That is truth, said the king as ye say; for it was I myself that came in the likeness, and therefore dismay you not for I am father of my child, and there he told her all the cause, how it was by merlin's counsel. Then the queen made great joy when she knew who was the father of her child.
>
> – Malory 1996: 4

In this situation the manner of conjunction is rather different and exceptional. Queen is acting in the capacity of the object and the subject. Therefore, the process of delimitation of experience is generally complete in her and the fact of curiosity is felt right at the place where queen launches herself into the scene of correlatives. In such an instance, she appears to be associating herself with a bare framework of ideas. Her conception of motivation is not to conceive a form of content rather to elevate and decline into an insignificant bottom where no correlative is to be found. She can neither move towards left to retain a primacy of truth for herself, nor is she in a position to turn on her right to accept the authority of goodness for her. This situation is such a situation in which the options for her movement are finally closed and the disintegration of two important determinants of meaning truth and virtue are formally closed. She cannot even negotiate or defend her honour, hence she has to inaccurately enter into an alliance with illusory formation, therefore, she repels an obviously virtuous perception and recruits in her conduct something that terminates her. The temperament of association declines an open activity for the sake of truth and honour, and it begets a situation in which we are forced to ask as to how dissociation (death) could be an event of participation (such of instinct as queen undergoes with an unknown visitor). The matter of presentation is not conclusive whereas it is basically recourse for the sake of abstraction and also for the sake of losing the sight of a basic form in which there is only truth and truth. The utterances define an exact place for constantly reducing and ever reducing formation of queen into absolutely a meaning for abruption, and, for that matter, these are the opposites which are added to the event of nonsense. The situation in that way would close the terms through the following manners of projection:

$$(\text{Queen})\ A = a^{-}\ a^{--} = a^{---}.$$

The structure of crisis presents informal notion of involvement and engagement, yet characters concerned do not appropriately receive the construction of hope and enthusiasm as parts of growing desire. This leads to the creation of non-acceptance in the hands of the queen herself who proposes herself for dissociation and enriches herself through the same dissociation. The play and interplay of illusion and disillusion destroy the worth of meaningful situation.

The constant interface of appearance and reality creates a place for the creation of meaning through conjunction. In this situation the scale of involvement in association is maximum and total. For example in *Betāl Paccīsī*, we have the following situation:

> द् च (त) मन्त्रिपुत्रेण तेन रहसि तस्मं दुश्पापांशंसता समाश्वासित स्टयक्त धैर्य्यः प्रोवाच - "सखे! यस्या नाम न् ग्रामो न, अन्वयश्च नावबुध्यते सा कथं प्राप्यते? तन्मृषा मां किमश्वासयसि?" । इति राजपुत्रेण (य) उक्तो मन्त्रिपुत्रस्तमम्य धात् - देव! कथं न द्रष्ट्रं त्वयां यत यत तया संज्ञया सूमिंतसपमेज? यत्तया कर्षो उत्पलं न्यस्तं तेन् एतत् सूचितं - करोप्पि लस्य राज्ञः राष्ट्रे अहं निवास्म्मीति । कृता च या दन्तारचना - यथाऽहं तंत्र (द) दन्तघाटकस्य कन्येति । शिरसि पहनं धृत्वा एतत् (घ) सङ्केतितं - यथादहं नाम्ना हृदयार्पितहस्तयां च तया, - त्वयि (प) चित्तप्रसादकः महासमृष्मिान् दन्तघाटकः सङ्केतितम् । अस्ति च कलिङ्गदेशे कर्णोत्पलो नाम प्रतिवसति तस्य कन्यास्तमियं पद्मावती नाम प्राणाधिवर्पि मम् एतत् लोकमुखात मया विदितम् । तस्मात् मया तस्याः (फ) देशादिसंज्ञा सङ्गिनी संबा ज्ञातां । इतितेन मन्त्रिपुत्रेणोक्तो राजपुत्रः ।
>
> *d ca (ta) mantriputreṇa tena rahasi tasmaṁ duśpāpāṁśaṁsatā samāśvāsita sṭayakta dhairyyaḥ provāca – "sakhe! yasyā nāma n grāmo na, anvayaśca nāvabudhyate sā kathaṁ prāpyate? tanmṛṣā māṁ kimaśvāsayasi?" । iti rājaputreṇa (ya) ukto mantriputrastamamya dhāt – deva! kathaṁ na draṣṭaṁ tvayāṁ yata yata tayā saṁjñayā sumiṁtasapameja? yattayā karṣo utpalaṁ nyastaṁ ten etat sūcitaṁ – karoppi lasya rājñaḥ rāṣṭre ahaṁ nivāsmmīti । kṛtā ca yā dantāracanā – yathā 'haṁ tantra (da) dantaghāṭakasya kanyeti । śirasi pahanaṁ dhṛtvā etat (gha) saṁketitaṁ – yathādahaṁ nāmnā hṛdayārpitahastayāṁ ca tayā, tvayi (pa) cittaprasādakaḥ mahāsamṛṣimān dantaghāṭakaḥ saṁketitam । asti ca keliṅgadeśe karṇotpalo nāma prativasati tasya*

> *kanyāstamiyaṁ padmāvàtī nāma prāṇādhivarpi mam etat lokamukhāta mayā viditam | tasmāt mayā tasyāḥ (pha) deśādisaṁjñā saṅginī saṁbā jñātāṁ | ititena mantriputreṇokto rājaputraḥ* – Prathama Kathā

Structure of inquisition is based on a permanent projection of illusion and wonder, and, therefore, the person (the Lady, the Prince and his friend) make out a total involvement into the situation. The beauty of the Lady initiates a proposal for alliance through the love, and, the Prince at the first sight does not come to terms with this, to compound the situation with further action, the Lady initiates a series of gestural action to conceptualize the terms inherent in her proposal. The resultant sign system upholds a refined and purer shade of conviction, and, in each, one could see complete and total meaning. For example: to suggest her nativity, she points at the ears' meaning thereby that she lives in a province whose name is Karṇotpala, then she indicates her gesture of teeth and makes out immensely clear that she is born in a place whose name is Dantaghāṭaka. Further, she suggests her name by moving her feet, which means to say that her name is Padmāvatī, and finally points her heart explaining her love for him. Thus, although, the Prince did not understand yet she sustained the mood of love and romance by associating him with realistic form of wonder and illusion. This is to say that, for him, the beautiful Lady, her love for him, and her manifestation of this love through imploratory sign system are all the parts of the larger system of seeing and believing/seeing and not believing, hence this tendency of himself into the situation through a location within wonder and illusion. It would also mean that the three persons, who are involved in this, can be rightfully equated to stop any further separation of anyone from the situation. The love and romance are the activities which the action of the situation creates and in these two, the primary methodologies of associating and excellently transforming oneself would become the best form of conjunction. This becomes evident while we understand that woman is at the highest form of assertion and the Prince and friend are at a comparatively lower scale of comprehension. Woman (Padmāvatī) becomes an authority, through whom the structure of meaning as the sign is communicated, organized and synthesized, and subsequently deciphered. The primary groundwork of this brilliance of activity suggests how the terms and condition gradually develop into a final form. The position of Prince is that of an ineffective wanderer whose strength and ability are no more than an infant, in that he could see but not found the worth of structure in his sight. His friend, on the other hand, is wise and therefore could interpret the circumstance, and could also turn an obviously failing situation into a glory of success.

The narrative begins on a promise of association and alliance, and, hence it makes out a series of inclusive forms, and inclusive terms and conditions. To suggest this idea, there is a definite pattern of strength occupied by each of the characters. The Lady, therefore, is maximum and the highest in relation to the presentation of a structure of meaning by composing a discourse of curiosity and illusion in the manner of an excellence of reality. Effect of comprehension is not obtained by the Prince as it should have been, and consequently, he is made to lack an expression for the curiosity to internalize the synthesis of illusion. The idea of calling the formation of relative conditions as situation of reality offered through curiosity and effect of illusion is precisely based on the assumption that the object as well as the event are circumstantially deprived in assuming a synthesized framework for the character, before whose eyes the offers appear and tend to devolve on him. To this extent, the Lady appears and quite convincingly confuses the Prince for her love, and, on the other hand, Prince associates his strength of comprehension to his friend and turns the whole situation into something that is really relational in effect through form and manner. However, the wholesome effect of the entire narration appears to be very permanent in view of the fact that the conjunctions are realistically transformed to create a depth of presentation for each of the readers. There cannot be any variation in the situation being primarily genitive. The purpose of obtaining a coherent shape for the projection of wonder is to initiate recognition of one's own curiosity in relation to the dilemma of association and non-association. The three figures of variation are relatively inclined towards constructing a full-length assertive conjunction hence the manner of falling in love dissociates the actual acceptance and defers it through a discontinuity. Nevertheless, the humanistic vision and purpose cannot uphold the tendency to be effective in the circumstances of truthful illusion. The extension of an objective form rests on intended disappearance of thoughtful perception. For this reason, the daughter of the King, the Prince and the friend of the Prince are changed into the composite model for them. It is only the Lady, who does not change or exchange the manner of presentation, the other two constantly keep changing and exchanging themselves, and, on that account, one character constitutes the core, while two others only supplement this foundation. The practical needs of the formal situation would suggest a growth along the connecting coordinate. The best aspect of the whole situation is that the characters keep up an enthusiasm about themselves and therefore they become so keenly interested in the position which the existing circumstance has made for them. The effect of conjunction is felt all along as the existence of the character and the precise reason why the beautiful Lady is engaged and involved with the Prince, and why and how friend of Prince is so keen to connect him to the cousin of Prince. Answer to this question ultimately leads to the recognition of the fact that they are relationally interdependent and create a flat mechanism of interdependence. Conjunction in effect is a property that could well be explained through this form in this context.

In the *The Canterbury Tales*, the cast of characters and their frames of mind are so penetrating and so vast that they undoubtedly enlarge themselves through a succession of immediate forms and immediate manners. In the Knight's Tale, for example, the progress of the situation is realistic to the extent that truth, reality and fiction are functionally operative (the characters: The Knight, Thesius, Palamon, Arcite, Emily) continue to develop action through abrupt events, and discontinue the promotion of native terms. Even in this rather odd formation of action in character, the brilliance of thematic perception is continued and maintained.

*The contrarie of al this is wilfulnesse.*
*Why grucchen we? Why have we hevinesse,*

*That good Arcite, of chivalrye flour*
*Departed is, with duetee and honour,*
*Out of this foule prison of this lyf?*
*Why grucchen heer his cosin and his wyf*
*Of his wel-fare that loved hem so weel?*
*Can he hem thank? nay, God wot, never a deel,*
*That bothe his soule and eek hem-self offende,*
*And yet they mowe hir lustes nat amende.*
– Chaucer 1958: 87

Chaucer presents a committed form and confirmed manner of inquisition through which he suggests an association in which object and subject both are repeatedly transmitted and transformed. The manner of suggesting this interrelationship is through a constant reliance of attitude on each other. Emily and Arcite on the one hand, love and the experience of love, on the other hand, and Knight as an authority, on still other hand, make up the constitution of this associative form. There is no facility to promote an exercise of mutual recognition, rather the author disengages the underlying situation from the eyes of the character. The fundamental question is of trust and hope. The question that is being asked is related to the way of being convinced about the very circumstances of life contained in the art of achieving conjunction as by displacement of both the object and the subject. The movement of the object displaces Emily and Knight so much so that the relative equations of knowledge and power both change. Love is come up both in the manner of shock and hope, therefore, through this opposition we have a conjunction in persistent appeal to the bond that unites an individual with the familiar situation, and events and action. In this narrative episode, we are brought nearer to an aggregate of an involvement into an experience so that both bring correspondence and take us away from the normal perception of love as an experience than a style of achieving, love has resulted in the loss of Arcite and the character concerned is now hopelessly mourning the whole situation. This could be well understood in developing and constituting a situation in which relativity of an experience is projected as an addition to the strength of the character. At the same time, the perception is built around the regeneration of primordial experience like love and hate leading to the resolution and reassessment of the past disappointment and future hopes to become important aspects in understanding the nature of action mounted on the individuals. It amounts to saying that the continuity of time with an assertion of a fact or a part of experience is basic qualitative condition that deals with the constitution of the character. If it is possible to say that the genesis of action motivating an experience was *A* and continuity of the same situation through revived enthusiasm is now *B* the graphical projection would constitute coordinates along the lines of a circle.

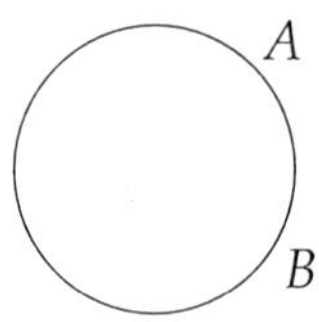


The manner in which character finds an opportunity to carry out narrative action is really something that one must appreciate. Death of Arcite is a sequence of perceptible motion for the flow of meaningful contents and the points opted for such an exercise are primary as the expressions with a feeling of involvement that created warmth and the secondary association that now leads to reconstruction of the same consciousness of delight and enthusiasm. The invocation of an attitude to finally sum up the urgency of an experience is one of the basic features of Western narratives. To present this form of expression some possibilities are generally sustained. In the first place, the individual is brought to an acquaintance with a personalized form of sensation in which the sensation is always degraded, and second, when this acquaintance is intensified the individual does not find himself in a position to fully receive the rather extraordinary presentation through morbid sensation. The role of conjunction in such a system is expected to be the medium to prolong the stay of an individual in those experiences, which he considered to be more appropriate than the others. Looking at the two situations, it seems quite possible to enlarge the scope of discussion by saying that the individual or form himself or herself goes on extending the length of perception by disembodying the geographical prolongation of his/her own existence. For example, in *The Decameron*, we have the following:

> Before thou art more familiar with me hearken to what I have to say to thee. As thou mayst perceive, I am no man, but a woman. Virgin I left my home, and was going to the Pope to obtain his sanction for my marriage, when, as Fortune willed, whether for thy gain or my loss, no sooner had I seen thee the other day, than I burned for thee with such a flame of love as never yet had lady for any man. Wherefore I am minded to have thee for my husband rather than any other; so, if thou wilt not have me to wife, depart at once, and return to thine own place.
>
> – Boccaccio 1951: 83-84

The nature of inquisition established in this narrative episode is well in line with the arguments advanced in the foregoing. The characters are consciously determined for the sake of an alliance whose sole basis is the discomfort that the stretch of experience brings. The idea of love does not mean to suggest an involvement rather it means an engagement that is absolutely for the purpose of acquiescing the benefits caused by the sensory imperceptions. This is to suggest that, on the either side of attitude, the strength of experience is only for the sake of benefit or gain or loss that it might bring otherwise there is no motif of understanding.

## IX

The position of conjunction contained in the form and even occasion is always based on the way in which we could extend the various divisions occurring in narrative events. It is entirely the work of involvement and commitment or even association to hold up a meaning in both the beginning and end of the situation. In *Kathāsaritsāgara*, for example, the effect of conjunction is a necessity in making the entire framework very homogeneous and really graduated for the sake of multiple associations. Look at the following:

> नगरं न प्रवेष्टव्यं युष्माभिरिह साम्प्रतम् ।
> यतो वल्लभशक्तिः स विपन्नोऽत्र महीपतिः ॥

दत्तो विक्रमशक्तिश्च राज्ये सम्भूय मन्त्रिभिः ।
प्राप्तराज्यः स चान्येद्युः कालनेमेरगाद् गृहम् ।।

श्रीदत्तः क्व स ते पुत्र इति चामर्षनिर्भरः ।
तमपृच्छत्स चाप्येनं नाहं वेद्मीत्यभाषत ।।

प्रच्छादितोऽमुना पुत्र इति तेन निषूदितः ।
कालनेमिः स शूलायां राज्ञा चौर इति क्रुधा ।।

*nagaraṁ na praveṣṭavyaṁ yuṣmābhiriha sāmpratam* ।
*yato vallabhaśaktiḥ sa vipanno 'tra mahipatiḥ* ।।

*datto vikramaśaktiśca rājye sambhūya mantribhiḥ* ।
*prāptarājyaḥ sa cānyedyuḥ kālanemeragād gṛham* ।।

*śridattaḥ kva sa te putra iti cāmarṣanirbharaḥ* ।
*tamapṛcchatsa cāpyenaṁ nāhaṁ vedmītyabhāṣata* ।।

*pracchādito 'munā putra iti tena niṣūditaḥ* ।
*kālanemiḥ sa śūlāyāṁ rājñā caura iti krudhā* ।।

– *Kathāsaritsāgara*, p. 138

In this situation, the act of narration is coincidental and concomitant to the individual experience hence the inquisition, and curiosity; wonder and surprise occasion a momentary correlation with an undetermined consequence, therefore, the individuals, their experiences of the event, and the resolution, both are functional with regard to the resolution that is developed through an inconclusive situation. At the beginning, association between the subject and the object is brought about by an advice through necessary imposition or even command, yet is further made unstable and inconstant in that both the object and the subject enter into a framework of negotiated settlement by approving the indetermination and effectively bringing about a resolvable formulation through composite attitude. The situation grows to an intensity of recognizing the potential of inquisition on both of the sides. It must be stated with conviction that the object and the subject correlation in the earliest situation is based on approval, disapproval, recognition, derecognition, acceptance, unacceptance so on and so forth.

The facts contained in the conjunction are quite satisfactorily explained through admission to the situation and expulsion from the situation. Vikramaśakti is forcefully halted just for the sake of an act of compliance elsewhere. In other words, we can say that by not entering into the situation, Vikramaśakti adds to the prevailing circumstances because situation is decreasing virtually. On the one hand, Kālanemi is slained just on the assumption, and, on the other, there is likelihood that Vikramaśakti will meet the same fate, if he desires admission to the situation. It would mean further that entering is an entrance that is symbolically a defect that has come up to the situation and the defect is principally a circumstance of rejection. The suitability of the situation adds to the extreme urgency that allows Vikramaśakti and others to homogeneously and effectively participate in the situation. It would mean that association is enriched primarily because keenness of involvement that is felt with concern and warmth. Vikramaśakti is relative to Kālanemi and therefore one who informs Vikramaśakti not to enter into the situation is primarily a relative conjunction in which mutual relations are called upon to meet so as to rotate through convergence of attitudes.

In *Kathāsaritsāgara*, the aptitude of character is committed to the mention of necessity and requirement in terms of safety and sanctity of individual projection and because of this Vikramaśakti realizes the motivation issued by the emerging conjunction. There is primarily a unified series of linear coordinates for elevating the dignity of conscience and choice of Vikramaśakti to evoke wholesome attitude from the coherent symbols and, for the purpose, he could consider the abolition to reversible modes of sympathetic attitude, and sympathy cannot be considered to be the right version of forming a manner of association, for example: *A* cannot always be in a position to be correlated with *Aa* and *AA* – because of the reason that supplementary forms may have aberrations in receiving the authentic expression, and, for the purpose, margin could be seen to be in the making by the virtue of difference hence the equation will be facilitated through inverse addition and inverse multiplication. The ability of an individual to understand the difference in homogeneous perception and the dispersal when experience is the part of his movement towards abbreviating the most important conjunction for him and in this regard, he could either perform a large-scale deformation for him so that he could finally enact a kinetic form of inception and reception of whole situation. This is one of the primary notions in the prevalence of an individual over action. In the following narrative episode, there is a truthful orientation of the process of committed deformation and subsequent enrichment. Look at the following:

बभूव रूद्रशर्माख्यः कश्चन ब्राह्मणः पुरा ।
बभूवतुश्च तस्य द्वे गृहिण्यौ गृहमेधिनः ।।

एका सुतं प्रसूयैव तस्य पञ्चत्वमाययौ ।
तत्सुतोऽपरमातुश्च हस्ते तेनार्पितोऽथ सः ।।

सा च किञ्चिद्विवृद्धस्य रूक्षं तस्याशनं ददौ ।
सोऽपि तेनाभवद्, बालो धूसराङ्गः पृथूदरः ।।

मातृहीनस्त्वयायं मे कथं शिशुरूपेक्षितः ।
इति तामपरां पत्नीं रूद्रशर्माथ सोभ्यधात् ।।

सेव्यमानोऽपि हि स्नेहैरीदृगेव किमप्यसौ ।
किं करोम्यहमस्येति साप्येवं पतिमब्रतीत् ।।

नूनमेवंस्वभावोऽयमिति मेने च स द्विजः ।
स्त्रीणामलीकमुग्धं हि वचः को मन्यते मृषा ।।

बाल एव विनष्टोऽयमिति बालविनष्टकः ।
नाम्ना स बालकस्तत्र संवृत्तोऽभूत्पितुर्गृहे ।।

असावपरमाता मां कदर्थयति सर्वदा ।
वरं प्रतिक्रियां काञ्चित्तदेतस्याः करोम्यहम् ।।

इति सञ्चिन्तयामास सोऽथ बालविनष्टकः ।
व्यतीतपञ्चवर्षोऽपि वयसा बत बुद्धिमान् ।।

अथागतं राजकुलाज्जगाद पितरं रहः ।
तात द्वौ मम तातौस्व इत्यविस्यष्टया गिरा ।।

एवं प्रत्यहमाह स्म स बालः सोऽपि तत्पिता ।
वां सोपपतिमाशङ्क्य भार्यां स्पर्शेऽप्यवर्जयत् ।।

*babhūva rūdraśarmākhyaḥ kaścana brāhmaṇaḥ purā* ।
*babhūvatuśca tasya dve gṛhiṇyau gṛhamedhinaḥ* ।।

*ekā sutaṁ prasūyaiva tasya pañcatvamāyayau* ।
*tatsuto 'paramātuśca haste tenārpito 'tha saḥ* ।।

*sā ca kiñcidvivṛddhasya rūkṣaṁ tasyāśanaṁ dadau* ।
*so 'pi tenābhavad, bālo dhūsarāṅgaḥ pṛthūdaraḥ* ॥

*mātṛhīnastvayāyaṁ me kathaṁ śiśurūpekṣitaḥ* ।
*iti tāmaparāṁ patnīṁ rūdraśarmātha sobhyadhāt* ॥

*sevyamāno 'pi hi snehairidṛgeva kimapyasau* ।
*kiṁ karomyahamasyeti sāpyevaṁ patimabratīt* ॥

*nūnamevaṁsvabhāvo 'yamiti mene ca sa dvijaḥ* ।
*strīṇāmalīkamugdhaṁ hi vacaḥ ko manyate mṛṣā* ॥

*bāla eva vinaṣṭo 'yamiti bālavinaṣṭakaḥ* ।
*nāmnā sa bālakastatra saṁvṛtto 'bhūtpiturgṛhe* ॥

*asāvaparamātā māṁ kadarthayati sarvadā* ।
*varaṁ pratikriyāṁ kāñcittadetasyāḥ karomyaham* ॥

*iti sañcintayāmāsa so 'tha bālavinaṣṭakaḥ* ।
*vyatītapañcavarṣo 'pi vayasā bata buddhimān* ॥

*athāgataṁ rājakulājjagāda pitaraṁ rahaḥ* ।
*tāta dvau mama tātausva ityavisyaṣṭayā girā* ॥

*evaṁ pratyahamāha sma sa bālaḥ so 'pi tatpitā* ।
*vāṁ sopapatimāśaṅkya bhāryāṁ sparśe 'pyavarjayat* ॥

– *Kathāsaritsāgara*, p. 230

We could see that the primary meaning created by heterogeneous experience intending a constant deformation and makes out a proposition that individual form will have to receive the difference created by an exceptional addition and subsequently he will have to receive a truth for perception. In this context, Rudraśarmā, the chief protagonist, happens to be the formation in which there is a reasonable choice of the preferences, and because of that he observes a judicious presentation of the judgement. The act of perception for him is supposedly the enrichment of truth because of the fact that he definitely understands as to how differential circumstances would lead to the disappearance of the content of reason. In this episode, son and wife become nominal agents to conduct very successfully the process of deformation. This structure of deformation is precisely the way in which optimum choice through selection is obtained. For Rudraśarma, the wife is stylistically inoperative because she could interact the functional

The Character (Rudraśarmā)

↓

Formative Principle (Deformation)

↓

Intensity of Inquisition

↓

Deviant Formative Perception

↓

Heterogeneous Formative Inquisition

↓

(Wife)

*Supra-deviant Inquisition*

You are my husband and you should go by me?

You should believe in what I say?

What I say, is what you ought to think and act?

(Son)

*Enriched Deviant Inquisition*

Am I not your son?

Am I not worth your affection?

Am I the one whom you care most?

Am I the one for whom you can disengage your present wife?

Am I the one for whom you can dispense with everyone and everybody?

↓

Enrichment of the Individual Form

↓

Truth

↓

Universality

**Chart 1**

model with dysfunctional abstraction contained in the idea she is expected to be carrying out. She doesn't like the first son of Rudraśarmā from his earlier marriage, hence she could deviate the contents precisely and regularly, and in the process, she could also disengage the term of movement meant for each one of them. Rudraśarmā is a beginner and primary face of the action that is mounted on a part of truth and a part of intention. Son to Rudraśarmā is intermediate conjunction whose affiliation to the evidence is correlated to the position of certainty and acceptance. It is possible to see that the act of believing in the truth of action is merited on account of realistic acceptance and a generous commitment for the sake of appearance.

The scale of appearance for Rudraśarmā, his son and his wife are basically different. In Rudraśarmā, the terms of acceptance are absolutely concrete, and therefore, he prevails upon both in constituting a meaning for truth. There can be a position of authority in the manner in which Rudraśarmā conveys his willingness to understand the basis of fundamental inquisition through another perceptible sequence of genitive interaction, and, in this regard, his formal primacy in relation to his son and his wife becomes the evidence of his movement into the ground of inquisition. The beginning for this has been continuous since the son asks him to be tough and hard with the mother and ultimately it is all resolved into distinct formative events (see Chart 1).

In this way we can understand that the relative importance of inquisitive perception supports the view that the narrative association and the movement of medium in a coherent narrative event are systematically rotated for an ideal formation. Rudraśarmā's evolution as a necessary truth by deforming a part of his own individuality and the whole of son's and wife's individualities is factually illustrative of the position.

In one of the earliest European narratives, *The Decameron*, there is enough opportunity to find consequence of resolvable inquisitive models and the point is always upheld that individual or form, having a relative terms of association with the projection of intensity, is liable to be displaced with a committed motion for the creation of a sequence of change tending to bring about the resolution. For example, look at the following episode from *The Decameron*:

> Then, as the friar was about to give him absolution, Ser Ciappelletto interposed: "Sir, I have yet a sin to confess." "What?" asked the friar "I remember," he said, "that I once caused my servant to sweep my house on a Saturday after none; and that my observance of Sunday was less devout than it should have been." "O, my son," said the friar, "this is a light matter," "No," said Ser Ciappelletto, "say not a light matter; for Sunday is the more to be had in honour because on that day our Lord rose from the dead." Then said the holy friar: "Now is there aught else that thou hast done?" "Yes, master friar," replied Ser Ciappelletto, "once by inadvertence I spat in the church of God." At this the friar began to smile, and said: "My son, this is not a matter to trouble about; we, who are religious, spit there all day long". "And great impiety it is when you so do," replied Ser Ciappelletto, "for there is nothing that is so worthy to be kept from all impurity as the holy temple in which sacrifice is offered to God." More he said in the same strain, which I pass over; and then at last he began to sigh, and by and by to weep bitterly, as he was well able to do when he chose. And the friar demanding – "My son, why weepest thou?" "Alas, master Friar," answered Ser Ciappelletto, "a sin yet remains, which I have never confessed, such shame were it to me to tell it. . . . Know, then, that once, when I was a little child I cursed my mother;" and having so said he began again to weep bitterly. "O, my son," said the friar, "does this seem to thee so great a sin?
> – Boccaccio 1951: 29

The variety of inquisitions obtained in the curiosity of perception make out a concrete and strengthened form of conjunction situation. It is to be understood that direct comprehension of an indirect event is normally a circumstance through which the position of authority is brought to the recognition of the individuals, and, therefore, constructs a gradual assertion and reassertion in the manner of concentric reception of context and the medium. In these given utterances, the nativity of assortment through primary model of conjunction is strongly inbuilt. For example, through an inward formation in the manner of an absolute inquisition and total reception, the following form of sequence would emerge:

*A* Yet

↓

What?

*B* Yes

↓

Is there ought else that than last done?

*C* Come

↓

What is this that than sagest?

## X

In these artistic formations, the sanctity of virtue performs a necessary mutation in both thinking and sensibility, and, therefore, a natural flow of experience maintains a rather smooth growth of both inquisition and perception, and that is how the narrative constructs, the ideas of truth and meaning for the purpose of exposing every event/situation to the strength of inherent categorical formation.

2

# Injunction

In the earliest narratives, the expression of contents generally occupy a position of certainty and distinction, and, therefore, manner of expression and style of perception of content are only suitable to the largeness of content and, in fact, the reality that could be seen to be validated, achieves the highest form of presentation. The character or form or individual, who comes to express itself, has a purpose in finding a series of those objects which ultimately create bases for their perpetuation in the context, governed by the medium of the narrative. This is to say that injunction appears as an effective system of correspondence when both the object and the subject are completely transmuted so as to create an equitability of contents in the external and internal media. The strength of injunction lies in the fact that it could interact with a form and position. The objects, which are supposed to be falling into the perspective of change, tend to be inscribed by themselves in those situations in which the strength of context is the determinant of the communication of the medium. Conjunction is offered as a preliminary evidence in supposing an act of correspondence in which the formation of absolute is maximum and the succession of refined motive is almost committed to regular interaction. This situation obtains the following cyclical form:

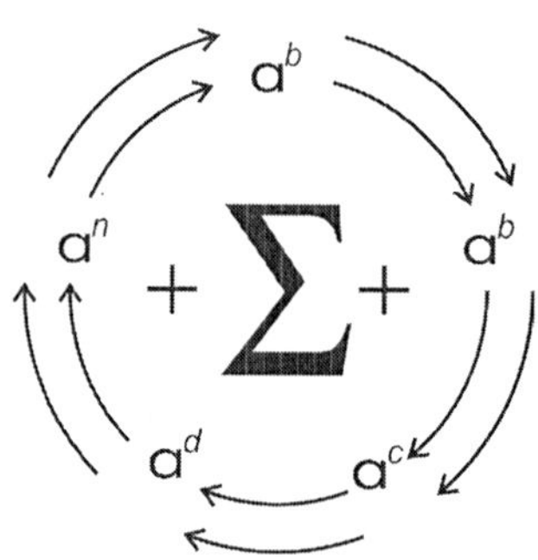

In this formation the degree of rotation of a content is almost equal to the intensity of enrichment, therefore, every content rotates by almost a perpendicular turn, while at the same time, there is no regressive deviation from the degree of rotation and because of this the position of content becomes very authoritative. This could also prove the point that the expressed part of the content opts for a complete change into the realized part of the content, accordingly, in the universal absolute (Σ) the rotatory terms are reinvented with a newer form of assortment and for this reason all turn in Σ itself. It is, in a way, amounts to recycling the formative part of the whole concept and bringing together the different part in such a way that each individual content becomes conclusive in itself. The normal length of an injunction is prolonged till the process of absorption of medium into content and content into medium is complete. It is, therefore, actually confirmed that the significance of the actual situation and consequence of resolution both are adopted and approved with the help of a typical transforming agent. The preliminary function of an injunction is to become a thoroughgoing revival of the content of refinement so that resolution could be meant to be actually felt in the whole process. An injunction begins with the movement of content towards truth and reality and ends up generally with the effective admittance of both truth and reality as being universal parts of the whole situation. To situate an event of transformation in between conciliatory parts of the content is supposed to be a rather different task, and, for the same reason, there cannot be an event that could divide the content of primitive strength and the immediate strength of any given content. An event that builds up this situation will obviously have two most authentic variables in the form of intermediate subtractive and additive factors. Thus the action that would proceed towards an expansion either in the direction of subtraction or addition must undergo a change to achieve the similar length and cycle of prolongation and growth. To enrich this length of growth along the line of transformation, objects are supposed to have a facility to create specific coordinates like conjunct instruments and even cohesive coordinate in such a way that intensity of artistry should be accomplished and assimilated right at the point at which intention to induct the coordinate was made. This particular situation constantly builds up a fact of curiosity and intensity, and is identified as such in each and every object internally and externally. In Indian and Western narrative traditions, the morphology of injunction has been very significantly established through direct transformation and idealized universalization. In each of the cases, the primary importance of injunction is very successfully retained, for example, in *Kathāsaritsāgara* we can have the following event contorting the identity and necessity of objects. Thereby, purporting a change as an effect of interdependent concretization:

तं व/यितुमिन्द्रोऽथ कृत्वा श्येनवपुः स्वयम् ।
मायाकपोतवपुषं धर्ममन्वपतद् द्रुतम् ।।

कपोतश्च भयाद् गत्वा शिवेरटमशिश्रियत् ।
मनुष्यवाचा श्येनोऽथ स तं राजानमब्रवीत् ।।

राजन्भक्ष्यमिदं मु/कपोतं क्षुधितस्य मे ।
अन्यथा मां मृतं विद्धि कस्ते धर्मस्ततो भवेत् ।।

ततः शिबिरूवाचैनमेष मे शरणागतः ।
अत्याज्यस्तद्ददाम्यन्यन्मांसमेतत्समं तव ।।

श्येनो जगाद यद्येवमात्ममांसं प्रयच्छ मे ।
तथेति तत्प्रहृष्टः सन्स राजा प्रत्यपद्यत ।।

यथा यथा च मांसं स्वमुत्कृत्यारोपयन्नृपः ।
तथा तथा तुलायां स कपोतोऽभ्यधिकोऽभवत् ।।

*taṁ va/yitumindro 'tha kṛtvā śyenavapuḥ svayam* ।
*māyākapotavapuṣaṁ dharmamanvapatad drutam* ।।

*kapotaśca bhayād gatvā śiveraṭamaśiśriyat* ।
*manuṣyavācā śyeno 'tha sa taṁ rājānamabravīt* ।।

*rājanbhakṣyamidaṁ mu/kapotaṁ kṣudhitasya me* ।
*anyathā māṁ mṛtaṁ viddhi kaste dharmaṁstato bhavet* ।।

*tataḥ śibirūvācainameṣa me śaraṇāgataḥ* ।
*atyājyastaddadāmyanyanmāṁsametatsamaṁ tava* ।।

*śyeno jagāda yadyevamātmamāṁsaṁ prayaccha me* ।
*tatheti tatprahṛṣṭaḥ sans rājā pratyapadyat* ।।

*yathā yathā ca māṁsaṁ svamutkṛtyāropayannṛpaḥ* ।
*tathā tathā tulāyāṁ sa kapoto 'bhyadhiko 'bhavat* ॥
– *Kathāsaritsāgara*, p. 108

The model of resolution, adopted in this event, anticipates the transfer of conjugal and concomitant inferences. There is a king in whose lap, all of a sudden, a pigeon falls which, in turn, was chased by a falcon – both pigeon and falcon have changed their beings and are in fact the gods themselves. They are out to find if the king on whose lap the pigeon is fallen is really worth the name and fame that he has earned. The king, now, does not allow the falcon to kill pigeon and the falcon was very angry and asks for compensation from the king by offering his own flesh to the falcon. The quantity of flesh was to be equal to the weight of the pigeon. King went on cutting the flesh and putting the flesh on one of the side of the balance. The other part of the balance, on which the pigeon is sitting, remains heavier yet the king went on cutting and putting his flesh on the other side. Here we can understand that the act of presentation is very expressive inasmuch as the reasonable assertions are quite pragmatically exposed for the sake of enrichment. The method of communication by identifying the object in each of the subject is significantly very systematic and regular and one has to admit the fact that the king as a subject becomes primarily the event of equality. King suggests a concern for an attitude that is recreated through the position of speculation. Such urgency really commits a factual inquisition almost entirely in the falcon and the pigeon and the king, hence they are substantially reconstituted and reaffirmed. This truth is very assertive here because of the fact that the falcon expounds himself in a greater conceptual depth and says:

राजन्भक्ष्यमिदं मु/कपोतं क्षुधितस्य मे ।

*rājanbhakṣyamidaṁ mu/kapotaṁ kṣudhitasya me* ।
– Ibid., p. 108

The intensity of regeneration has a qualitative movement and makes a strong suggestion of the fact that the objects of truth are sufficient to revive a situation for the object. The movement of assertion is logically evident in the idea of effective presentation. The king could understand the pigeon's lamentation and saved it. First, because of the fact that the king could invent in her urgency for communication. It is, in this regard, the displacement and replacement of the traversed field and acquired field both allow the king to accomplish a suitability of content for himself. Another important fact that is evident in this event is how the resolution of hypercritical assertion is brought about.

The purpose in maintaining an exact constitution of the contents is precisely to suggest a turn of universalization for the king, the pigeon and the falcon. Inasmuch as the style of approval and manner of suggestion both are casually aggravated through a definite conclusion just for the fact that the pigeon is now a God, the falcon is now an enlarged God, and, on account of the blessings of the both the king is also included into the hierarchy of the divinity. It would mean that every native form in the conditions of exceptional enrichment produces a supplementarity of constitution of exact variant, and, for this reason, the upgraded variant becomes an index of presentation and perception. The qualification of a supposed equality of the contents resulting into extra enrichment of the primordial form could become a normative act of communication, and, in fact, in the event suggested in the foregoing, the acceptance of earliest sensation formulates a similarity in the authoritative principle of convergence. The affirmation of a constant renewal could also generate a primary version of a superior excellence in the manner in which the reception of exceptional model of exposition has identified individual with a curiosity of communication, therefore, king's kindness enhances the movement of eagerness, keenness and finally builds up a condition in which he himself becomes a coordinate for the assimilation of the inherent condition. The more important part of comprehension that could be built around the whole solution is quite naturally the way in which the internal strength leads to the vertical exposition of the whole contour of the individual form, and, therefore, the following equation-specific arrangement of the content substantiates the scheme of presentation:

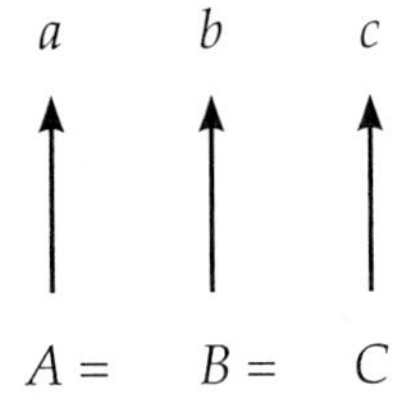


In this arrangement the larger variables designated by *A*, *B*, *C* are capable of giving rise to supra modes of enriched formation in the manner of *a*, *b* and *c*. And, on this account, we can understand as to how the king who freed the pigeon from the falcon is, in fact, creative of multiple inventions of the form. The circumstance of intra-invention and the correspondence of their invention to supreme form of induction rationalize the whole process of formation of assertive categories within the narrative event. The scale of precision that is formed as a rule in the process is introduced to the version of renewal. In other words, we can say that there is always a consistency and uniformity in presenting the extraction of variants within the given form. Even in *The Decameron*, the idea of continuous reinvention has been substantiated at length. In one of the events the attention is invited to the following situation:

> How am I to know, madam, that in your selection of lovers, you are not equally eccentric? In which case I should be the man of your choice, and the rest would be cast aside. Where to the gentle lady, somewhat same stricken as were also her fair friends, thus made answer: "Master Alberto, our presumption has received from you a most just and no less courteous reproof; but your love is dear to me, as should ever be that of a wise and worthy man. And therefore, saving my honour, I am yours, entirely and devotedly at your pleasure and command." – Boccaccio 1951: 63

In this event we can understand that curiosity and inquisition both are occurring at a very definite place and they acquire a conscious configuration, and, for that matter the process of conversion of an inquisition into resolution is equally very high. Master Alberto obtains a formal method to subject interrogative content to an extremely rich consequence of presentation and this he could revive both in himself and the queen. It is quite appropriate to say that Alberto's wisdom sharpens the strength of invention from within and once this process of invention is complete, he could easily externalize his authority. This methodology is further comprehensible in the reception of motive generated in the queen herself. She could only accommodate the length of enrichment suggested by Alberto and just becomes a part of the whole resolution phenomenon. It is very significant that the two characters are being preferred as a consequence of the lengthening content rather than application of a heightened medium on them. This continues the potential of actual interaction and the procedure of relocation has very sound bases in the whole event. Alberto's stand to the effect that he will have to attribute the content is formally stopped thus he enacts a number of modifying events beginning with an inception throughout, and, in that way, he completes the exclamation with inbuilt and assured models of radical perception. In this regard it appears to be only an excellence of the discourse that both the characters (Alberto and the queen) are brought to a fairly equal level of enrichment. It does not matter as to how and why the renewal of inquisition smoothly develops an event of change or an act of inquisition into an act of resolution. This would be the condition of a characteristic authority of artistry that we can quite easily comprehend.

The approval of a mature and developed object of comprehension brings about a logical change of intermediate situations, and, for that matter, any event that has completed its half cycle of typical formation will be added to the next constituents as a matter of fact or as a matter of rule. In each of the cases, we can understand that the growth of the narrative event would be very symmetrical and perfect. This situation could lend yet another solemnly intensive regulation, in that the portion of observer would be simultaneously compounded and confirmed in the object of consideration in such a way that the division of intended object would be actually assorted through two equal yet substantial propositions and the natural cause of growth would be from the position *A* to the variant of *A* and then the movement will be redrawn and revived through the variants of

*A*. In a continuity of development, the triangle of regular, cyclical and linear arrangements of terms are sometimes anticipated as a part of a scheme of displacement. In *Kathāsaritsāgara*, the scale of fixing up an arrangement of events is normally by projecting the content to its triangular coordinates and then reversing the movement for a cyclical interception and in that way there is a rich strength of variation between the received contents and the communicated part of the objects. There might be a greater inter-functional approval of rotation on account of this very scheme of operating continuously and as a part of motivated perception. This is not to say, on the other hand, that there is a loss of empirical forms, and there is a gain of abstract significance rather, of such movements, we can at large think of an intense resuscitation of the narrative events so as to resolve the whole part of the events. In the preceding situation, we had an appropiate resolution of the only subject inasmuch as the falcon stated his inquisition through an extensive realization, and said:

श्येनो जगाद यद्येवमात्ममांसं प्रयच्छ मे ।

*śyeno jagāda yadyevamātmamāṁsaṁ prayaccha me* ।

– *Kathāsaritsāgara*, p. 108

While at the same time the king offered to exchange and consolidate the function of empirical forms through his contention to the effect that:

तथेति तत्प्रहृष्टः सन्स राजा प्रत्यपद्यत ।।

यथा यथा च मांसं स्वमुत्कृत्यारोपयन्नृपः ।

*tatheti tatprahṛṣṭaḥ sansa rājā pratyapadyata* ।।

*yathā yathā ca māṁsaṁ svamutkṛtyāropayannṛpaḥ* ।

– Ibid.

The conviction of opting an injunction as a referential supposition through certain relative contents and in each relative content the proportion of resolution has consistently increased. For example, character or form or an individual enhances the motivation of inquisition of inverted/oblique contentions, and he will have an optimum chance to prolong the scale of effect and in that way the forthcoming resolution will be synthesized in almost all the directions of inquisition. The realistic part of methodology of resolution, naturally, acquires a projective certainty through the essential facts available in the medium, and, for this reason, in *The Decameron*, the male and female forms are always getting reduced yet at the instinct of reduction in them is an open-ended possibility of finding a conclusion to the presented merit of the situation. The effect of resolution changes the empirical conditions of the object and the subject. This seems to be very important, and we can examine this point as to how the radical concentration of pragmatic forms are juxtaposed in a series of ulterior deviances brought about quite successfully in such an act of change. In the two streams, which are in a position to respond to the space, there could be possibility of practical empiricism directly introduced by the tendency of the category to multiply form within. It does not matter now as to why the attributive scale of enrichment has been subjected to the deviance in refinement rather very advancing form cumulates and retains the meaning generated within. In this case, the worth of finding an immediate significance of the situation will almost be a practical reality and would be within the worth of inquisition. The evolution of the attitude of modification of content yields a variety of proposition therefore the character formation under the prescription of a situation acts and behaves in each a way that the entire form is changed into the external correlatives which regularly indicate the extent of acceptance and submission. This part of transformation is carried on with the help of lateral margins, and character/forms are available only through external content and, for this reason, whole of the two events are indicated as the optimum situation. The opposition between the content is never direct rather it is turned towards the lateral margin after having traversed the distance through linear progression. The possible inclination is on the right of the event and then successively the left margins are recovered. The suitability of position is also generally a matter of choice rather than of the power of artistic situation. In the following event in *The Decameron*, we can understand the manner of finding right and left intention by the virtue of an acceptance of empirical forms as the ultimate destination:

> On his answering that he was the man, she took him aside and said: "Sir, a lady of this country, so please you, would fain speak with you". . . "Andreuccio is here". . . bursting into a flood of tears, she kissed his brow, and in slightly broken accents said: "O! Andreccio welcome". . . "Andreccio, I can not doubt that thou dost marvel both at the caresses which I bestow upon thee, and at my tears, seeing that thou knowest me not, and, may be, hast never so much as heard my name;. . . grew so intimate with him that a child, was born, which child am I, thy sister, whom thou seest before thee.
>
> – Boccaccio 1951: 93

Boccaccio presents the significance of the situation in the manner of both reception and communication. The whole fact is incidental to curiosity and surprise, in that the characters are not in a position to approve the quality of the conduct of temperament and the strength of reality is such that it forces the lady and Andreccio to find a correlation to present the fact of communication. It is quite interesting to see how the compulsion of circumstance changes the relative position of the characters and an extent to which Andreccio is diminished by the virtue of interposed insufficiency of the content while the lady is revived in strength through an addition of the contents. This could be explained logically and comprehensively as to how the experience constitutes a nominative function for Andreccio, while it generates and organizes an inbuilt strength for lady character. Andreccio's slyness to meet the lady with uncertain motive does not indicate any virtue of his movement towards the organized content rather it is a graduated reduction by forcing each of the ultimate contents to break and deviate. It would be better to state the formation by identifying a conjunction assertion in this character in view of the fact that the real motive does not find any concentrated injunction in the situation. The application of injunction will be in excess of importance and would raise the qualitative loss, suffered in moving and advancing. The lady consumes conformity to the reality, and, for that matter, she organizes and attaches herself to the proximity to the reality, no matter how and why she could make her intention very clean. She has to get the money Andreccio is having, and to get the money she expresses herself through interpersonal form. In the whole event, the concept of dysfunction through organized association is suggested, and this has been achieved quite properly through affirmation and the imposition of affirmation on the extra functional forms of recognition. There is another way to find out a worthy position leading to the functioning of resolution event by mutating and interacting the formal functions of association between Andreccio and the lady. On occasions, it might suggest a position of elevation in which the constituents are constantly enriching themselves, while, on the other hand, the native, local, and universal forms are getting regularly disintegrated. It is to be seen that there are two active constituents which obtain maximum movement with regard to the reliable significance. Andreccio is formally indisposed to sustain the condition of truth and therefore falls prey to receptive/accumulative act proposed by the lady, and, on the other hand, the lady, being cunning from the heart deforms the shape of visible content. Any action that comes forth could not view the proximity of the situation through speculation or through inception. The only way that may be invented would be to render the whole structure of conformity to be very concrete, and, for that matter, we will now propose the substitution of contents from Andreccio, the lady must disintegrate the opposite side getting suitably enriched and for that matter transfer of progressive content from *A* to *B* and the reception of the similar contents from *B* to *A* would comprehensively equalize the aberration noteworthy in the given situation. Even otherwise it would be seen that the position of participant in the narrative event is unfortunately heterogeneous and generally decadent injunction carries the relevance of total methodology, for this reason, every injunction supports and sustains a normal form for itself. When it is expanded, it leads to reversal and when contracted it would ultimately implicate the terms through normal dissociation of the parts in which exterior and ulterior position of the content are considerably affected.

It now seems worth the while to examine certain conditions, which operate exclusively at the position of resolution and the precise effect of the relevant position is that the movement of content is intentionally and deliberately controlled. The first important part of content that comes to our recognition is inverted concentration, and, in the second place, we have varied concentration, and the third and the fourth segment of resolution are occupied respectively by upward concentration and dispersed concentration. The structure of narrative in an ideal or genuine circumstance is so much so that the adequacy of actual movement is required to be brought in for significant assessment of actually realized terms, and, for that matter, the exact and perceptible sequencing of events is absolutely worthy of the following generative equation:

$$\sum = A \times a = A/a = A - a.$$

The proposition so stated affects a sequence for truthful imitation of the various variables randomly found and randomly associated in consequence of eventual correlation brought at length by a pragmatic systematization of upward events. The advancement of a variable in a linear direction would invent aggregate types of factual assertions which are open for addition, subtraction, division and multiplication in accordance with the intensity of enrichment that it would carry. At the same time, the inversion of probable sequence merited for expansion or contraction would go side by side with the adoption of above arrangement. In the narration, the process of exposition of actual contents is made in accordance with fixed or coherent condition of acceptance, and, for that matter, the injunctive intensity intends to acquire an additional form for itself thorough the growth of formal contents. It is not very difficult to understand that the assortment of the participatory contents continues to be a rich potential till the time the action of event is introduced thorough any alternative or every relative form of correlation. It is apparently based on an idea that the association of resolvable parts is brought about by the cohesion of absolute situation, and, for this reason, in *The Decameron*, nearly every event foresees a compulsive loss or gain only thorough the fixation of a relative content in the margins. Unequal displacement of one absolute creates a noticeable variety of perception so as to induct a series of complimentary positions of effective assertions, and, because of this, when the characters/forms propose an alliance via association, they opt for an exclusive internalization of the whole situation. There can be considerable inversion of local contents in relation to the function of an action in initiating and activating a process of change through conjugal forms. This manner of forming a correspondence would actually mean how the listener is finding a measure of suitability of contents which were disposed for the sake of him only, when two characters are standing in cohesive relationship, we can merely perceive that the interaction and signification would assimilate the absolute part of content only. The activity that is presented for the sake of revival or resumption of the forms of association between the characteral kind could be understood to be the continuity of perfect, concrete, and complimentary retention of the meaning only.

The actual conditions leading to the creation of an injunction may be compulsorily associated with the continuous revival and release of absolute variants in the form of a purely concrete exchange of existential forms, a realistic upgradation of the immediate figural form of the character, the extensive evolution of the expansive form located in the external environment and the complimentary intra-associative index of perception attested in the functional part of existence. It must be an authorization for the sake of large-scale effects of the smooth growth of individual experience that the character communicates through a round and rotary variable. For example, in *The Kathāsaritsāgara*, the independent formation always begets a methodology for a superior and perfectly enriched version of induced codes while the dependent characters, which work out their intention only through the independent form suggested in empirical compulsion to resume the credit terms substantially by abrogating themselves. In *The Decameron* and *The Canterbury Tales* the effect of consummation is equal to the scale of association, and, therefore, the combined effort is large scale and carries the material index to the strength.

The outward stretch of a characteral form presented through either reflective or objective perception of a concentrated reality would obviously lead to the simultaneous functioning of the several parts of the environment. The intensive nature of such an aspect will be to review the advancement of actual conjunction which nearly forms a continuum with regard to the enrichment of the whole situation. In *The Canterbury Tales*, for example, the various characters are exposed in an extraordinary communicative urgency to adjust and accommodate universal function that might be a variant of the whole situation. In real terms, the extension of unit, universal to the whole universe, would be almost like finding a coherent scale location for a particular character. When we consider how wife of Bath reinvents herself in almost all the functions of communication endowed on her by the urgency of the situation. Exposing her in various men, while, at the same time, reviving herself through aggregate of whole of the man could be the wisdom of performance thrust upon the wife of Bath. In no other condition of action, we can understand the availability of a character in its external association. Injunction could variously be internalized as the form of expressive and communicable intentions having a property of outward and inward addition through the immediate necessity of transformation. The facts opt for an inclusion in the following events in *The Pilgrim's Progress*:

> Man: "I am now a man of despair and am shut up in it, as in this iron cage. I cannot get out. O, now I cannot."
>
> Christian: "But how comest thou in this condition?"
>
> Man: "I left off to watch, and be sober. I laid the reins upon the neck of my lusts. I sinned against the light of the word, and the goodness of God. I have grieved the Spirit, and he is gone. I tempted the devil, and he is come to me. I have provoked God to anger, and he has left me. I have so hardened my heart, that I cannot repent." – Bunyan 1969: 39

The process of determining the upward consequence of projection is quite curiously made to be associated with the possible non-variants of the situation, for this reason, man, as a form and character, speaks through implicative functions as we can understand when he says "I am now a man of despair and am shut up in it"; here the proposition is built around the fact of addition that ultimately is involved into the whole of presentation and for this reason we have to find special possibilities through "I am" and "am" both balanced and weighed in accordance with the length of condition that they could carry hence the term of resolution is the greatest. The creative model implanted and internalized form of continuity make out the coherence of attitude and perception. "Christian", one of the principal characters in *The Pilgrim's Progress,* finds an opportunity to regulate the primary condition so well and so absolutely that there is no deviance that can be seen or recorded. In Christian's terms, the internal function of virtue is more affirmative than the external part of the situation, therefore an individual form tries to correlate oneself with the universal in such a way that effective virtue is noticed and recognized as something that is universal. One must appreciate the cause and the effect of the invention of opening index in a complicated and invested utterance "I" and "am", and thus the length of displacement of character in these two final identities would be understood to be as maximum. It is of course better to conclude that the consequence of properties that is approached as model solutions converges while these variables fall outside the terms of injunction.

The idea of affirmation holds ground in the creation of injunction simply for the reason that the formation of similar magnitude of enrichment in two differential models would require a precise and balanced form of the models and content in such a way that each is in a position to presuppose only a formalization of associated facts of comprehension in the exposition of the character to the external reality or internal necessity of procuring a change/changeability or even a modification for the sake of survival. The character is raised consciously with the open-ended gaps in its form, and these gaps are meant to be filled up by him only. Regressive character and adjusting character both formulate a condition of extensive exchange of the realistic contents by interposing the corresponding manner of advancement in the external space system. A character/form is supposed to undergo rapid changes so as to befit the scheme of life and the fitment is a necessity of bringing forth proportion and fine balance between the logic of perception and the reality of exposition. It is sometimes believed and understood that the process of convergence is supplementary to actual revival of the character in natural form, which brings interesting results when truthfully examined. In *The Decameron*, for example, the basic condition that creates the character is not how they present themselves to the ethics of the emerging situation rather the force of context induces on them the logic of deformation to the extent that private needs of the character and the actual needs of the circumstances are so immensely juxtaposed that the relevance of the private self is lost immediately and as a result the natural self could be seen to be forthcoming. It is always at this point of impersonal constriction that we can understand how the functional part of the character is brought to the actual presentation. For this reason, every character conceives at least principle conjunction of reason to form a continuum or continuity for himself. It must be understood that men and women, and, for that matter, priests, traders, Barons, Knight, Squaire, landlord, Queen, rich lady, whores and others induct into them the richest part of injunction, thereby the ability to concretize is immediately comprehended, while in *Kathāsaritsāgara*, the predominance of choice as a virtue of presentation to the external world is remarkable. Every character (men and women including kings and queens; traders and artisans; firemen and beggars; princes and princesses; outcastes, prostitutes) conforms to the externality of the situation by the virtue of their existence. To this extent, the idea of negotiating a form prior to themselves and after themselves would hold well and the expressive intention of the situation would conclude the following system:

$$^{-a} = A = {}^{+a}.$$

The actual effect of conceiving of rational form for an effective display of the strength of characterization through its reinvention as an object conveys the sense of authority and significance, and anything that establishes a bond between primitive type and the recent expression could be understood as a rich principle of association. In any event, the effect of composition of a form is supposed to be excluding the replication of the value. To compliment this event, majority of functional forms are brought in a simultaneous correspondence and simultaneous exclusion in such a way that the activity of content within the form is absolutely fixed and contains the ability to display the credits it has obtained and acquired during the course of its movement from proximal universal to the proximal absolute. We can understand at the same time that the chance of injunction is not entered into the manner of digesting sequence of realizable modifiers rather it is manner of presentation that always draws upon enriched object capable of being associated and being changed. The penury effect obtained in conjunction is to locate the exact position of external and internal values of the idealized objects which act as modifiers thereby to bring about a condition of association through complete transformation. In Indian and European earliest narratives, a large variety of holistic as well as fractional event could be found and discovered, which will explain and illustrate how the events earliest suppose and dispose a dissented sequence of object for the sake of modification, in that each object so acquired and so changed will definitely bring about a condition of comprehensiveness in the narrative acts.

# 3

# Inception and Conception

## I

In the earliest narratives, the evidence of resolution is indicated in conformity with the adopted and acquired value through exceptional modification of the contents. Such an act of presentation and creation of meaning, is, accordingly, called inception or conception. In inception, the meaning is ideologically determinate because of the fact that substance of contention is adequately filled into the scheme of realization, and, for that matter, the nature of emerging concept is always free for the sake of an association and further correlation. The necessity of adopting a model of inception and conception as two interrelated yet extraordinarily rich versions of meaning formation could be a point in comprehending the earliest narrative. The application of conjunction principle in which defined object qualifies a designated subject, injunctions explain earliest narratives in that the function of comprehensive model leading to creation of adopted value becomes a basis of upgrading the manner of internalization and analysis. Only the idea of having a complete modification of plot or character as the very act of convergence could be intended, where we can obtain necessary ground for presumption of the situation. In plots, especially the acquisition of value is contained in the methodology in which reference to the object amounts to be the achievement of not only better communicative equivalent but also the extension of the suggestive part of the content. Referential contents direct all values in a movement. Composition of an event is in a state of continuous expansion and moreover the continuity of association brings about newer variants and models for the propagation of an ideal. In a character, content is supposed to invent the ethics of an event along with the idea of having a factual scheme for the correspondence with the external world is very developed, and when, the character goes onto approve or deny whatever he could come across as a part of his own extension. It would thus mean that it stands out as the authority behind the emergence of plot as a unitary system while the events in a plot cumulate and fix acquisitioned value for the sake of themselves. The other side of the situation intends to factually disorient the logical possibility of receiving a set of realistic object for the sake of perception. For example, in *Kathāsaritsāgara*, we can understand the situation:

> का त्वं रोदिषि कस्माच्च पृष्टा तेनेति भूभृता ।
> सा तं प्रत्यब्रवीदेवं मन्मयाज्ञानुवर्त्तिनी ।।
>
> यो वराहः प्रविष्टोऽत्र स दैत्यौऽगरकाभिधः ।
> अहं चैतस्य तनया नामागरवती नृप ।।
>
> वज्रसारममश्चासौ राजपुत्रीरिमाः शतम् ।
> आच्छिध राज्ञां गेहेभ्यः परिवारं व्यधान्मम ।।
>
> *kā tvaṁ rodiṣi kasmācca pṛṣṭā teneti bhūbhṛtā ।*
> *sā taṁ pratyabravīdevaṁ manmayājñānuvarttinī ।।*
>
> *yo varāhaḥ praviṣṭo 'tra sa daityau 'garakābhidhaḥ ।*
> *ahaṁ caitasya tanayā nāmāgaravatī nṛpa ।।*
>
> *vajrasāramamaścāsau rājaputrīrimāḥ śatam ।*
> *ācchidha rājñāṁ gehebhyaḥ parivāraṁ vyadhānmama ।।*
>
> – p. 166

In the sequence of perception, both the object and the subject (character/event) adopt a note of apprehended reality inasmuch as the strength of character lies in the fact that he could retain his presence through communicated expression. In fact, the girl, the king and the demon are the important forms, who are supposed to be conveying the sense of apprehension. The girl, who appears before the king while the king is bathing, in fact marks herself only because she is afraid and fearful of her father who has now got changed into the form of a wild pig. He may kill the girl, therefore, the girl is to be saved. In this outline, we can understand that theme of communication and the effect, wonder and surprise are so precisely built up that there is practically nothing that is wanting in the structure. The effect is unitary, and, therefore, among the demon, the king and the girl, some kind of semantic relationship is faithfully observed. The demon, having been transmuted into pig, is now sleeping and no sooner than he would get up, he would kill the girl who happens to be his own daughter. Realizing this, the girl proceeds to the king who is bathing and supplicates him to save her life. In this situation of trust and mistrust; hope and fear; belief and disbelief, we could understand how the modification of character into its next figural form is geometrically possible. The girl, who supplicates, is also one who achieves the system and pattern of absolute by reducing the combination of heterogeneous experience and thought content. She develops complete notion of amalgamation of the form. If it is well appropriated, she would no longer be fearful rather she will have truth of life around happiness and comfort, or, on the other hand, she would also find an arrangement for his valour and might inasmuch as he worked towards rescuing her from the imminence of danger. The third party, who is demon himself, is undergoing the erasure and to reincarnate himself in his extreme form, he will have to be sustained by the king. The whole pattern of characterization is such that each is sustained by each. This facility suits to the effort in which manners of mutual inception become a way to understand the fact that the nature of meaning derived from coalescence when there is an imposition that is really very vivid. In the above example, we have already seen how the act of transference not only revolves and solves the correlative conduction rather it also creates the conclusive selection for the purpose. Every such act for the purpose would end up in wonder or surprise. In earliest narratives, the interdependence of the contents expected to be so great that it is immediately considered to be expressive as a matter of extreme invention. The freedom of a character to locate the possibility of such a correlation could be necessarily dependent on his/her ability to propose critical function for himself in *The Decameron*:

> The lady answered: "I expect not, nor is it possible, that another should be more tender of my honour than I am myself. Were my parents so, when they gave me to you? I trow not; nor mean I to be more tender of their honour how than they were then of mine. And if now I live in master sin, I will ever abide there until it be pestle sin." – Boccaccio 1951: 169

In this circumstance the lady and the master are engaged into conflict resolution, a part of which is confirmed with the lady and the rest is shared by the master. In resolving the conflict, the lady accuses the master of having been so unworthy of himself and also unsuccessfully tried to fulfil the needs due upon the youth or age while she discloses the truth, she makes up her mind to homogenize the attendant conditions by exclusively speaking of the fact that the difference between youth and age is perennial and eternal, and, therefore, cannot be bridged. The sensations of the body have various forms and each form in itself is a signifier, while we try to correlate the signifiers we proceed to get the result in the form of the meaning. In the case of the lady, the signifiers are so portending and convulsive that she is practically forming an excess of her categorical contents. The man who is standing before her is certainly so marginalized that he cannot invent or create the equal terms for credit.

The actual purpose in withholding the truth of the matter lies in the fact that the object and the subject, which are engaged in pursuit to contain themselves for the sake of meaningful orientation, bring about diverse media for the expression, the husband of the lady does not intend to accept the ideal form rather he invested himself in the shifting logic of uncertainty. The lady, on the other hand, retains the fervour by resolving her through truthful equivalents; between them the question of deception has been equivocally ordained, accordingly, the wife advances further in associative form and the husband degenerates and disappears from the terms of signification. *The Decameron* continues with greater intensity, the separation, the quest of separation, the urgency of separation, the manner of separation between conception and inception. The scheme of arrangement has been so exact that one wonders how the question of severance amongst the multiple signifiers comes to explain the larger part of the action of the narrations. It must be stated at length that sensory lapses, committed as a rule in the growth of characterization, become the typical methods of portrayal of the given situation and the extent of idealization is so limited and so constricted that there isn't much scope of growth in the characters. It also, on the other hand, puts up a definition for a man being the man, and a woman being the woman. One understands that man is a man because he could deform the contents by confining himself to the purposive medium and hence in the object and context, accordingly, the ultimate worth of a man is in putting up a meaning on account of his excellence in lust. Similarly, a woman equally substantiates her projection via manifold recessions with the aim just to locate her finality in her beauty only. Such a commitment confers an exquisite material strength to the large body of contention that transpires between masculine and feminine formation. Obviously the purport of such an exercise would be to handle the thematic forms through contractive idealization in which the concrete universal is rarely coterminous and wholesome. The motion of intention is to organize the various centres of signification so as to balance the contents of assertion. In one of the similar circumstances, Boccaccio (1957: 83-84) tells us in *The Decameron*:

> Which the abbot speedily divined, or else surmised from some movement on Alssandro's part, and, laughing threw off a chemise which she had upon her, and taking Alssandro's hand, laid it on her bosom, saying: "Alssandro, dismiss thy foolish thought, feel here, and learn what I conceal." Alssandro obeyed, laying a hand upon the abott's bosom, where he encountered two little teats, round, firm and delicate, as they had been of ivory; whereby he at once knew that 't was a woman and without awaiting further encouragement forthwith embraced her, and would have kissed her, when she said: Before thou art become more familiar with me hearken to what I have to say to thee. As thou mayest perceive, I am no man, but a woman. Virgin I left home, and was going to the Pope to obtain his sanction for my marriage, when, as Fortune willed, whether for thy gain or my loss, no sooner had I seen thee the other day I burned for thee with such a flame of love as never yet had lady for any man.

We could understand from this that the discursive term renders the subjective motives into excessively heightened forms, whose method and application purposely mount to the inquisitive freedom of sorts and kinds. The lady in question, who has been abducted and readily taken in as a wife by the abductor, doesn't agree to return her home even while the husband requests her to come back. The reasons are not too far to be sought and must be laid in the gratification of sensual pleasures which were otherwise never possible. What is brought to notice and attention is the extreme immediacy of synthesizing/contrastive meaning. The structures of meaning are so unequal that there is not a single content that could explain how the propriety of the female does indeed become the strength of her excellence. The causes inherent upon such a situation could be understood to be general functions of the methods of internalization of the compulsive circumstance before the character, and, in the present context, we could understand that the constitutive term appear to be so grossly devastating that the individual/form is generally helpless.

The contents of inception sometimes vary from the content to the context and context to the medium. In *Kathāsaritsāgara*, for example, the conviction to comprehend assertion of an attitude is so concentrated that the character himself becomes almost total and complete with regard to the impending events. The accomplishment of effect suggests a method of bringing about and presenting the facts of meaning through such concrete events that the realization is almost at once. The lengthening of object in relation to the subject is so significant that it is almost immediately brought into the environment of association, for example, look at the following:

तद्भयाच्च तदान्येऽपि नृपा वाच्छन्ति नैव ताम् ।
तदा सेनापतिं राजा निजमेव समादिशत् ॥

इतो देशात्त्वयैकैक: क्रमादेकैकतो गृहात् ।
पुत्रान् प्रत्यहमानेयो ब्राह्मण: क्षत्रियोऽथवा ॥

आनीय च प्रवेश्योऽत्र रात्रौ मत्पुत्रिकागृहे ।
पश्यामोऽत्र विपद्यन्ते कियन्तोऽत्र कियच्चिरम् ॥

उत्तरिष्यति यश्चात्र सोऽस्या भर्त्ता भविष्यति ।
गति शक्या परिच्छेत्तुं नह्यद्भुतविधेर्विधे: ॥

*tadbhayācca tadānye 'pi nṛpā vācchanti naiva tām* ।
*tadā senāpatiṁ rājā nijameva samādiśat* ॥

*ito deśāttvayaikaikaḥ kramādekaikato gṛhāt* ।
*putrān pratyahamāneyo brāhmaṇaḥ kṣatriyo 'thavā* ॥

*ānīya ca praveśyo 'tra rātrau matputrikāgṛhe* ।
*paśyāmo 'tra vipadyante kiyanto 'tra kiyacciram* ॥

*uttariṣyati yaścātra so 'syā bharttā bhaviṣyati* ।
*gati śakyā paricchettuṁ nahmadbhutavidhervidheḥ* ॥

– *Kathāsaritsāgara*, p. 336

In this we can understand that the king happens to bring about a thoroughgoing examination of the available condition so as to suggest a new model for the sake of realization. Thus the lady in question has been subjected to typical stages of graduation for the sake of her own enlargement in the context. The best thing that we can make out is the range and availability of choice so as to render oneself very significant in the given situation. It is not that only the vehemence or rage through desire coordinates and renders the important purpose and the effect of motive. The lady is given the opportunity to implicate in herself the range of additives, which will ultimately bring about strength to her. The intention to freely conjoin in the imperatives of freedom that really gives immense strength and applicable groundwork to the adequacy of her role as a subject of the discourse. She freely chooses the events and modifies them according to the necessity of the events, and further accordingly extends the communicative variants so much so that individual forms and their citation for the sake of certain purposes become at once imminent. The opening of the discourse on the note of a consequence in "तद्भयाच्च तदान्येऽपि नृपा वाच्छन्ति नैव ताम् । (*tadbhayācca tadānye 'pi nṛpā vācchanti naiva tām* ।)" and the closure that has been realized equally formidably in "उत्तरिष्यति यश्चात्र सोऽस्या भर्त्ता भविष्यति । (*uttariṣyati yaścātra so 'syā bharttā bhaviṣyati* ।)".

The conclusive events bring about harmony of order in establishing the fact that the external variants and the internal equivalents both are open for a conclusive orientation should the context, the content and the medium are generated in functionally aggravated condition. Extremity of concretization in establishing the point of fact in a rather contractive environment discredits the virtue of evolution and the consequential projection does not find any good meanings in the recorded situations, obviously the characters will undergo the loss of utility in the diminishing fashion. Nearly all the Western earliest narratives have convenience in highlighting this situation as the forms/characters fall upon the idealization of lust as a principle of conduct. In the seventh novel of *The Decameron*, the aspect becomes exclusive to the facts of comprehension:

> Day by day Pericone's passion waxed more ardent, being fomented by the proximity and contrariety of its object. Wherefore seeing that blandishment availed nothing, he was minded . . . this novel demeanour was by no means lost on Pericone, who saw in it a good omen of his speedy success; so, with profuse relays of food and wine he prolonged the supper far into the night. – Boccaccio 1951: 121

Here, it might be possible to bring to the notice the fact that the male and female, under examination, undergo a crisis in obtaining a worthy meaning for their instinctual fallacies. The male character has been overpowered by a massive rage consequently proceeds to the female for the sake gratification and ultimately prepares a ground for the communication of efficacy for such a purpose through advanced signifiers that the female is at once unable to comprehend the motive thus falls upon the error of inception. What we can understand is that the continuity of communication is, in other ways, an acceptance of enraged sensation by submissive woman, who contrives only to accord an acceptance to the creation of fallacy of instinct and recreation of the same fallacy into the subject is actually the model of perception generated in the context. Ability to perform in an immediate content to the extent of distortion could be found as a way to achieve heterogeneity, a condition considered to be so necessary to sustain the situation.

In Indian and European contexts, the manner of conceiving the circumstance for the sake of obtaining length and extent of conformity upholds the merit of greater and smaller composition of the structures of meaning. The aspect that invites our attention is now in Indian context the sensory perceptions/imperceptions, which do not disfigure the largeness of meaning. While in European context the indexing of individual/form into lust brings the essential signification of his or her action, which dissociates the condition of transformation, and, consequently, only in aberration we can understand how the contents are dissolved.

## II

The structure of meaning that comes up for evaluation in these two contexts has an exceptionally differential value with regard to association of conjunction. The term primarily refers to the effect of action upon individual/form and multiplicity of responses generated by individual/character to invent an ideal index. Index is numerically coherent and strengthened proposition that brings about the mutual agreement, adjustment, coordination and finally reciprocation. In European context, the function of an event and an action is to present the individual only, and, so far as he could understand what is circumstantially available to him. For this reason, the nature of the object and the subject participating in action is precisely the one in which each is constricted and limited. It would mean, in other words, that the position is always unequal to figural or formative authority included in the disposition. It leads, in the next place, to exclude all the positive forms and include nearly every constrictive figure. In *The Pilgrim's Progress*, for example, look at the following conversation between Christian and Apollyon:

> Christian: "Wherein, O Apollyon, have been unfaithful to him?"
>
> Apollyon: "Thou didst faint at first setting out, when thou wast almost choked in the Gulf of Despond. Thou didst attempt wrong ways to be rid of thy burden, whereas thou shouldest have stayed till thy Prince had taken it off. Thou didst sinfully sleep, and lose thy choice thing; thou wast also almost persuaded to go back at the sight of the lions; and when thou talkest of thy journey, and of what thou hast heard, and seen, thou art inwardly desirous of vainglory in all that thou sayest or doest."
>
> – Bunyan 1969: 59

The occasion substantiates the idea that the inability to prolong the largeness and efficacy of the context certainly goes against the characters hence the reason for primal imbalance lies not in the individual nor even in the form but in the sociocultural contexts that usurp the existential terms and forces the individual to devolve and manifest through smaller function in which he may have the feeling of association. But that is only an unreal proposition to constitute an assortment, and, what, in fact, it does is that it disorganizes numerical functions which are otherwise so strongly called for the purposive conferment. In the present context, we may understand that every correlative constitutes a process of devolution for Christian. One after the other he could find that he suffers a loss through the continuity of reducing content. It seems better to approach the understanding by assigning to the individual and the action, the conspicuous signifiers and thereby to analyse now each, in fact, stands in opposition to the others. Christian's denial of the charge that has been labelled against him becomes a figuration of the value codes in that it explicates both the sign and the signified. Biblically being unfaithful would be infidel, and being infidel consequently would be sinful, and one who is sinful is open for the punishment by God. Christian utilizes functionally operative signs to equal the adequate opposition that this sign would bring about. What happens further is that the corollary of internalization goes on absolutely dispersive. Thus none enters into any conjunction whatsoever. Sin of one is the punishment because of the other and thus the action mounts on the improbable coordinates. It would be slightly better to say that actions are purposive, in that the individual falls upon the aberration even while the procedure that tends to provide him some strength would have come to his rescue. The diversion of the probable absolutes into inward cleavages brings about disproportionate rising of the extent of figuration; accordingly, what we find is that the individual and action are separately accessible to the already diverged cleavages. Such a separation is almost entirely complete to situate the functionality of growth. It is almost questionable as to why and how separation comes in excess to the character's native strength. The answer to the question may have some analytical figures in that individual and action come very close to the functioning of random variables. Christian's imposition in this regard is an advancement to restore the conjunction for prospective expansion while Apollyon's counter position disallows and deforms the upbringing of equivalent variables. In *Hitopadeśa*, on the other hand, the form and action both expose and revive the conjunction and necessarily obtain the meaningful place in the totality of the situation. For example, look at the following instance:

> अस्ति चम्पकाभिधानायां नगर्यो परिव्राजकावसथ: । तत्र चूडाकर्णो नाम परिव्राट् प्रतिवसति । स च भोजनावशिष्टभिक्षास्त्रासहितं भिक्षापात्रं नागदन्तकेऽवस्थाप्य स्वपिति । अहं च तदस्त्रामुत्पुत्य प्रत्यहं भक्षयामि । अनन्तरं तस्य प्रिय सुहृद्वीणाकर्णो नाम परिव्राजक: समायात: । तेन सह कथा प्रसंगवस्थितो मम त्रासार्थ जर्जरवंशखण्डेन चूडाकर्णो भूमिमताडयत् । वीणाकर्ण उवाच – 'सखे! किमिति मम कथाविरक्तोऽन्यासक्तो भवान्?'। चूडाकर्णेनोक्तम् – 'मित्र! नाहं विरक्त: । किंतु पश्यायं मूषिको ममापकारी सदा पात्रस्थं भिक्षास्त्रामुस्लत्य भक्षयति।' वीणाकर्णो नागदन्तकं विलोक्याह – 'कथं मूषिक: स्वल्पबलोऽप्येतावद्दूरमुत्पतति? तदत्र केनापि कारणेन भवितव्यम् ।
>
> *asti campakābhidhānāyāṁ nagaryo parivrājakāvasathaḥ । tatra cūḍākarṇo nāma parivrāṭ prativasati । sa ca bhojanāvaśiṣṭabhikṣāstrāsahitaṁ bhikṣāpātraṁ nāgadantake 'vasthāpya svapiti । ahaṁ ca tadastrāmutputya pratyahaṁ bhakṣayāmi। anantaraṁ tasya priya suhṛdvīṇākarṇo nāma parivrājakaḥ samāyātaḥ । tena saha kathā prasaṅgavasthito mama trāsārtha jarjaravaṁśakhaṇḍena cūḍākarṇo bhūmimatāḍayat । vīṇākarṇa uvāca – 'sakhe! kimiti mama kathāvirakto 'nyāsakto bhavān?' । cūḍākrṇenoktam – 'mitra! nāhaṁ viraktaḥ । kintu paśyāyaṁ mūṣiko mamāpakārī sadā pātrasthaṁ bhikṣāstrāmuslatya bhakṣayati ।' vīṇākarṇo nāgadantakaṁ vilokyāha – 'kathaṁ mūṣikaḥ svalpabalo 'pyetāvaddūramutpatati? tadatra kenāpi kāraneṇa bhavitavyam ।*
>
> – *Hitopadeśa*, p. 48

The constituents of action support the homogeneity of both the individual and the consequent event in such a way that there is a regular correspondence between the object and the subject. The hermit, who has kept the food in a certain place and the food is being eaten by a certain rat provides an excellent groundwork for the perpetuation of an action. The conjunction, at once, brings about the necessity of the mutual adjustments and thereby the action makes itself so open-ended and so formalized that meaning becomes directed upon the competence of wholesome action and situation and that is precisely how to keep the food away from the approach of the rat. The significance could be located in the naturalization of the whole process and it is rendered into almost commonplace and practical experience akin to any of beings. What, in fact, has happened is that the conjunction which unites the form with actions reveal themselves through suggestive motives hence brings about surprise in every instance which in turn becomes the instrument of modification. The dissimilarity between the true traditions in the manner of conceptualization of the impending events has a good deal of the similarity. Inasmuch as Western situation, the event is resolved without having been idealized while in Indian context every event, or, for that matter, any of the events adds itself to a continuous and regular induction into simplification procedure. It seems to be somewhat difficult to assign reasons for the internalization of such an effect yet the systematization of value function could be the ground of exploration. In *The Pilgrim's Progress* and *Hitopadeśa*, difference is obviously because of the differences in assimilation of the index. In *The Pilgrim's Progress*, the rage is dissociative, whereas in *Hitopadeśa*, the similar rage is associative. The conclusion of such a nature would be an appropriate logic to describe the purpose and motive, inscribed in the narratives of two traditions.

## III

The accumulation of specific variables and the subsequent synthesis also has a committed role to play in the making of the actions of the earliest narratives. In Indian context, every action gives rise to figural propensity worthy of being described in such quantifiable terms as $a, b, c, d, e, m, f$ and randomly each is seen to be synthesizing so as to end up with final summation in $\sum$. The extent of synthesis has also certain noteworthy properties accordingly it is vertical, horizontal, lateral and intensive in that the division is brought about yet division is so conclusive and resolute that it enacts a mutation of itself with the addition of a range of structure and function. The structures and functions propagate an advanced additive contention so as to thoroughly synthesize each and every event. In the Western context, such a property is observable only through vertical and horizontal divisions hence the reception of those events, which have undergone cleavage, simply does not take place. While we look at the existing situation, the following equational arrangement in respect of the harmonization of action in the Indian earliest narratives would be uniformly observed:

$$\sum = a + b + c = d \ldots n.$$

This would suggest how the action is configured through the synthesis that is obtained in the addition of the various variables and the process of addition continues almost incessantly. The adequacy of quantification, of necessity, implies a definite manner of production of idealized form in the context of the situation in which the character moves to comprehension by discovering legitimate correlatives, consequently, affects such an arrangement. In the Western conditions, action is either vertically or horizontally distorted, in that the conjunctions dissipate abruptly and do not allow any addition amongst the context, however, even within the situation an equation could be worked out in the following manner:

$$\sum = (a/a^{-}) + (a^{-}/a^{-}) + ----n.$$

In this scheme of arrangement, we can understand that every action commences a series of regression so as to reduce and dissociate the properties of synthesis, and, at the end, what emerges is the extreme localization of the form and individual. This is precisely the way in which we can approach the understanding of the narratives under examination.

## IV

The occurrence of individual and the continuity of action are through the contrastive forms and characterize the methodology of inception in the earliest narratives belonging to these two traditions. In Indian context the meaning is a propensity, and thus it acquires ideal terms by the virtue of complete transformation of individual into actual and the vice versa. However, the corresponding situation in European context doesn't support the wholesome synthesis, rather it adds to the creation of those meanings, which are immediately comprehensible without having any further stay in the larger action. The smaller variants are precisely the facts, which signify the better pursuit of the action in these narratives. As inception is basic to the maturity of any action inherent upon the narrative purpose, it really does not generate any strength whatsoever for those contexts where the scale of modification is only immediately specified. Indian earliest narratives, therefore, find better application in reinvention and functionalizing the larger variants for an ideal configuration.

# 4

## Resolution and Convergence : I

### Pañcatantra and The Canterbury Tales

THE humanity is strength and richness of motivation of person or object towards fulfilment of both external and internal manifestation of the experience itself. It is a coherent and harmonious situation of building up a relationship with inverted imagination and the external thought. We can understand that when meaning is created on account of the above, we come to have the humanity. Therefore, chief characteristics of humanity would be understanding, sympathy, approval and acknowledgement because in each we have thoroughgoing meaning and whose purpose is to enable or elevate the dignity of the object or a situation, or an event, or even a form. There are two ways of understanding the humanity as a logical consequence of an experience. In the first place, humanity comes to mean the total strength of the object, and second, it is concerned with the evolution of logical structure and the category in the objects. In other words, we can say that the creation of an absolute is the fundamental ground work of humanity.

There is a necessity to balance the situation by bringing forth certain standards for our estimation and valuation of humanity. In the first place, it is necessary that the position and situation of the object and the event must be known thoroughly. On occasions, it may so happen that the object is not fully changed into an event, and, in that case, there can be no shade of humanity. Primarily, humanity is a feature of association, addition, growth, perfection, purity and refinement and, for that matter, it is something to do with the birth of soul in the human beings and that is why humanity is concerned with the human civilization.

## II

The idea of humanity in the form of understanding, sympathy, involvement and care has been at the foundation of the narratives in Indian and Western traditions. *Pañcatantra* and *The Canterbury Tales* are two powerful expressions of this situation. In *Pañcatantra*, the expression of humanity is total, complete, absolute and perfect, and, in a way, this grand text of narrative creates perfect forms of conviction, motivation, sincerity, fidelity and trust in such a way that each becomes a complete form in it. The narrative introduces sorts of characters which are quite convinced about the basic motivation of the mankind. That is to say that the creation of a standard of facilities for the life is built upon a rather natural, easy, convincing, real and homely circumstances, and, for this reason, presentation of different situation is absolutely unified and interrelated. In this section, Viṣṇuśarmā works out universal foundations for the life in the background of the study of loss and gain of sorrow, happiness, generosity, sincerity and recklessness in life. Each occasion of success is quite reversible through the failure that attends it and complete success will always have failure in its attendance, if recognized chain of event is reversed. What is needed is that the object should presuppose the strength of the opposite or diverse or unfamiliar or hostile objects and the like. In this regard, Mitrabheda of *Pañcatantra* is remarkable. The positive perception (knowledge and experience) about the absolute perfection envisaged into the characters is significantly present. The characters are normal and they enter through natural strength, association, order and harmony. The warmth of the life, or, for that matter, the mechanism of the life is object specific and action oriented. In the Knight's Tales, on the other hand, the strength of humanity comes as a consequence of an imaginable participation in an imaginary act to resolve the local condition. There is a situation in which largeness of the action is compounded at the beginning of the whole situation. It is to be understood that preliminary act in which the characters make the movement is precisely for the sake of a correspondence between fascination and wonder.

In the present situation the Knight (Theseus) and the two women at a later stage, Emily, Palamon conduct themselves into a formal situation in which the manner of expressing reality does not go hand in hand with the form of action, with which they are preoccupied. This is to say that separation of the object and the event is so great and so large that the character and action are only mechanically interposed.

In the Knight's Tale, we come to have a sight of the Knight, the women and the young lovers, and this sight leads to the war, in the first place, and wonder and amazement in the second. It is not that the Knight does not recognize the presence of this situation. It so happens that the situation recedes from both the ends. From the point of view of the subject and the object, the characters have little control over the situation. The main idea is that the humanity expresses itself and there is a keenness to procure the reward of unstable mental attitude.

In *Pañcatantra*, the characters approach a throughgoing understanding, absolute warmth and exceptional concern. In the early stages of its growth, it appears exclusively in the form of a meaning due upon the object and the subject, and the resolution of the object into an event for example. There is a monkey that loses the life simply because he was adventurous and full of enthusiasm, and could not pay any heed to the advices given to him. It means that the concern in this case is not only imminent in the object but in the situation, in which the objects are resolved. For that matter, an advice is given not to proceed further yet he goes, nail in the wood clutches him and he dies:

> एकच तेषां प्रत्यासन्नमृत्युचापल्यात्तस्मिन्नर्धस्फाटितस्तम्भे उपविश्य पाणिभ्यां कीलकं संगृह्य यावदुत्पादयितुमारेभे, तावत्तस्य स्तम्भमध्यगतवृषणस्य स्वस्थानाच्चलितकीलकेन यद्वृत्तं तत्प्रागेव निवेदितम ।
>
> *ekaca teṣāṁ pratyāsannamṛtyucāpalyāttasminnardhasphāṭitastabhe upaviśya pāṇibhyāṁ kīlakaṁ saṁgṛhya yāvadutpādayitumārebhe, tāvattasya stambhamadhyagatavṛṣaṇasya svasthānāccalitakīlakena yadvṛttaṁ tatprāgeva niveditam* | – *Pañcatantra*, Mitrabheda, p. 14

Here we can learn that the subject (the monkey) dies because of a mischief done by him yet the manner in which he is brought to this pass is really remarkable. He reaches the stage of inhabitation by the virtue of repeated and regular conduct of orientation performed on his behalf by the elders. He had been warned of the consequences yet he did not pay any heed to. Obviously, the story implies that the standards of resolving the practice into a form are absolutely concrete and perfect, for that matter, the involvement could save the whole situation. This aspect has other dimension, in that there is a reaffirmation and re-emergence of truth repeatedly, severally, variously, simultaneously, no matter how overwhelming the odds are, Viṣṇuśarmā is in a position to suggest that the endeavour of a weak is instant, immediate and at once, and therefore the sudden appearance of mistrust, distrust and suspicion does not really thwart the long and grasping foothold of the timeless and eternal trust of any individual. For example:

> अथ तस्य नृपतेर्गृहसम्माजनकर्त्ता गोरम्भे नाम राजसेवको गृहायातोऽपि तेनानुचितस्थान उपविष्टोऽवज्ञायाऽर्धचन्द्रं दत्वा निःसारितः । सोऽपि ततः प्रभृति निम्सत्रपमानास्त्रा रात्रावप्यधिशेते । 'कथं मया तस्य भाण्डपते राजप्रसादहानिः कर्तव्या' इति चिन्तयस्त्रास्ते। अथवा किमनेन वृथा शरीरशोषणेन ।
>
> अथ कदाचित्प्रत्यूषे योगनिद्रां गतस्य राज्ञः शय्यान्ते मार्जनं कुर्वस्त्रिदमाह - अहो, दन्तिलस्य महद् दृप्तत्वं यद्राजमहिषीमालिंगति ।' तच्छ्रुत्वा राजा ससभ्रममुत्थाय तमुवाच - भो भो गोरम्भ, सत्यमेतत् यत्त्वया जल्पितम् । किं दन्तिलेन समालिगितां' इति ।
>
> *atha tasya nṛpatergṛhasammājanakarttā gorambhe nāma rājasevako gṛhāyāto 'pi tenānucitasthāna upaviṣṭo 'vajñāyā 'rdhacandraṁ datvā niḥsāritaḥ । so 'pi tataḥ prabhṛti nimsatrapamānāstrā rātrāvapyadhiśete। 'kathaṁ mayā tasya bhāpate rājaprasādahāniḥ kartavyā' iti cintayastrāste । athavā kimanena vṛthā śarīraśoṣaṇena ।*
>
> *atha kadācitpratyūṣe yoganidrāṁ gatasya rājñaḥ śayyānte mārjanaṁ kurvastridamāha – 'aho, dantilasya mahad dṛptatvaṁ yadrājamahiṣīmāliṅgati ।' tacchrutvā rājā sasabhramamutthāya tamuvāca – bho bho gorambha, satyametat yattvayā jalpitam । kiṁ dantilena samāligitāṁ' iti ।*
>
> – *Pañcatantra*, Mitrabheda, pp. 45-46

Now it is possible to understand that the situation changes and brings about new awareness and new recognition of the ideas and the attitudes involved in the making of human perception. Accordingly, the King Dantila and Gorambha are caught in a situation in which there is a separation and emergence of the truth.

King is a standard, Dantila is an expression and Gorambha is a degeneration of an experience. When Gorambha tries to defunctionalize the opening of an experience by misleading the king about an untrue and unworthy fact, he also becomes, by and large, intermediate form because he is positionally unsuitable to bring about the resolution. Now the king enacts and goes onto expel Dantila just as a measure to protect his own privacy and individuality, and, at a later stage, in the story the resolution of the experience becomes a factual position, therefore, Dantila is brought back. It would mean that the king enjoys a throughgoing and full-scale involvement into the whole range of perception and it is precisely because this Dantila is detained as a corollary, correlative and equivalent of this class of perception.

The experience of being involved and being a part of the whole situation is thoroughly concrete in each of these hence the eyes of the king could foresee the genuine sympathy in Dantila and debunked abstraction of error in Gorambha. The point is how men arise and retain the privacy of individual and finally look into the largest stretch of his experience by looking at similar constructions.

In the Knight's Tale, we are led away by the motive of romance as the basis of individual consent and we ask a question as to how and why the ruthlessness of war could generate equal and approximate situation in love and romance. The opposition developed by the poet, is perhaps, less convincing than the opposition that one finds in the propagation and perpetuation of the romance itself. It must be understood that the story progresses on account of a supplication made by two women to Theseus, and, thereafter, there is joy at Theseus and Theseus succumbs at a later stage to the advances made by two beautiful ladies. Yet the act of involvement is an instrument to define and settle the enraged sensibility. Knight's position in the narrative is supposed to be superior to the other characters, and, therefore, he has been presented in such a way that he could be an absolute dictator.

The Knight is affected by a commitment and concern to present the individuality as a matter of negotiation, and, for this reason, he does not quite easily agree to marry her sister with either Arcite or Palamon rather he proposes an execution of the task for the purpose:

> *And this day fifty wykes, fer ne ner,*
> *Everich of yow shal bringe an hundred knightes,*
> *Armed for listes up at alle rightes,*
> *Al redy to darreyne hir by bataille.*
> *And this bihote I yow, with-outen faille,*
> *Up-on my trouthe, and as I am a knight,*
> *That whether of yow bothe that hath might,*
> *That is to seyn, that whether he or thou.*
>
> – Chaucer 1958: 53

It means that the form of understanding of others is based on definite standards, therefore, man could be presumed to be the man who is in a position to create an order of the value, accordingly, an experience shall have meaning. The various models of meaning, that the Knight is insisting upon, are a realistic framework for the examination of anybody is worthwhile. In this regard, one can understand that the fixation of authority, acceptance of authority and execution of authority remain the basic goals of the whole situation and surprisingly occasion and context for each is always immediate in nature hence external situations do not come to the rescue of either the Knight or other participating characters. This turns the whole situation into an abstract formation inasmuch as the immediate manner of composition of a situation that does not entail the execution of models from outside the world.

Human forms are intended to commit an exercise of change of motivation, perception or experience through the ordinary sets of everyday language and sign system, and there is also a compulsion to complete the formation within a frame of time fixed by the situation. This makes the characters to be slightly inexpensive and prone to general abstraction. In the present context if we could look at the Knight, and Arcite, and Palamon, we would definitely find that continuity and regeneration of occasion and situation do not extend a helping hand to either of them unless one is thoroughly abstracted as a term for value. The Knight conceives a greater form of recognition inasmuch as he puts forth realistic terms for the valuation and assessment of life. It seems as if the Knight is eternally fixed in a series of checks and balances. The will to introduce the sets of reformatory standard is compensated by an equal affirmation in the hands of rough models (Arcite and Palamon) with an imminent gap in modifying the resolutions. For the purpose of resolution Arcite and Palamon both did not succeed. It is now understood that in the Knight's Tale the presence of involvement has been graduated along in a series of disassociation and disintegration, for that matter, there is no immediate success in presenting the massive power of thinking and feeling. It so happens that the constant approaches to embody intensity of feeling is rebuffed through the violence of rage, for example, look at the following.

*Allas, the wo! allas, the peynes stronge,*
*That I for yow have suffred, and so longe!*
*Allas, the deeth! Allas, myn Emelye!,*
*Allas, departing of our companye!*
*Allas, myn hertes quene! Allas, my wyf!*
*Myn hertes lady, endere of my lyf!*
*What is this world? What asketh men to have?*
– Chaucer 1958: 79

The implication involved in the expression of rage is just that the characters are becoming hostile to the environment and because of that there is a great imbalance between perception and thought. Perception is an unusual imposition on an otherwise gentle frame of thinking and feeling. This imposition of wonder and curiosity somehow creates imbalance in the whole life. This is a new turn given to the action, and explanation for the situation may vary from enthusiasm to keep up oneself exactly in the way the life has brought up. It is not that Arcite or Palamon opting the truth rather truth, is now slightly deviated from the normal perception. In *Pañcatantra*, the effect of perception compels a motive of reality and significance, and, for that matter, there is a comprehension about both the immediate and eminent standards of life:

> अथ सजीवकसकाशमासाद्य सप्रश्रयमुवाच – 'भो मित्र, प्रार्थितोऽसौ मया भवदर्थे स्वाम्यभयप्रदानम् । तद्विश्रब्धं गम्यतामिति । परं त्वया राजप्रसादमासाद्य मया सह समयधर्मेण वर्तितव्यम्। न गर्वमासाद्य स्वप्रभुतया विचरणीयम्। अहमपि तव संकेतेन सर्वां राज्यधुरममात्यपदवीमाश्रित्योद्धरिष्यामि । एवं कृते द्वयोरप्यावयो राज्यलक्ष्मीर्भोग्या भविष्यति ।
>
> *atha sajīvakasakāśamāsādya sapraśrayamuvāca – 'bho mitra, prārthito 'sau mayā bhavadarthe svāmyabhayapradānaṁ । tadviśrabdhaṁ gamyatāmiti। paraṁ tvayā rājaprasādamāsādya mayā saha samayadharmeṇa vartitavyam । na garvamāsādya svaprabhutayā vicaraṇīyam । ahamapi tava saṁketena sarvāṁ rājyadhurama-mātyapadavīmāśrityoddhariṣyāmi । evaṁ kṛte dvayorapyāvayo rājyalakṣmīrbhogyā bhaviṣyati ।* – *Pañcatantra*, Mitrabheda, p. 44

Here Piṅgalaka and Damanaka are assessing the situation for the sake of their enlargement into the situation, yet by the sheer deformation of wonder and curiosity, resolution is withheld and the cause of this shift is Sañjīvaka, the bull. In this episode, the manner of consideration of apprehension is enactment of fulfilment and association with which Piṅgalaka is concerned. About his fellow being, he does not want to deviate the continuity of formal perception, and, for this reason, his thought becomes normally imperceptible to him. There is a gap between the reality in itself and its extension of the same to the outer universe. What is important in the situation is the endurance of a motive not to reflect upon the deviance and normality of conscience. The position of Sañjīvaka implies a realistic form of perfection in which the actual experience forms a motive in confidence or even the strength of the fellow being. In that way, the subjects in *Pañcatantra* grow along a model developed and erected by the inward experience, therefore, it is enlarged and universalized on each of the occasions. To the best of performance, the character is busy and engaged in pursuing a logic and conclusion of concrete events with the external world, therefore, he appears to be so large, so high, so big, so authentic and so great. The modification is absolutely the retention of the character in an event that is a noteworthy excellence of the whole situation. For example, the Sañjīvaka is not graduated to irregular, manifold and inconstant changes either in his form or in his event and because of this the primacy of narrative situation is established.

In Knight's Tale, conditions differ due to multiplied assertion of an inconclusive and indeterminate individuality. Theseus is subjectively in contrast with Arcite and Palamon and he goes a long way to prove the point that reward of virtue is not a matter of one's possession rather it is a succession of claims, rights and power. This is because of a factual worth in Knights' dispensation in award and reward of virtue. This appears to be rather inconclusive and inconvenient and raises a host of problems in pursuing the text.

The motives pursued by the Knights are effectively the enactments of power and authority which are procured in the manner of imposition. In other words, we can understand the whole situation to be as constantly leading to the extreme regimentation of the intensity built up by the artistic situation in the further growth of the story. Arcite dies away yearning for a romantic fulfilment yet there is no fulfilment as such. It is only Palamon, who stays back and wins the game. Look at the following:

*Then seyde he thus to Palamon ful right;*
*'I trowe ther nedeth litel sermoning,*
*To make yow assente to this thing.*
*Com neer, and tak your lady by the hond.'*
*Bitwixen hem was maad anon the bond,*
*That highte matrimoine or marriage.*

– Chaucer 1958: 87

This method of interposing and intercepting a resolution through deviant form is so unique in *The Canterbury Tales* that it becomes at once a formation of whole process of considering action and conducting the action towards the larger framework of the life. It is also one of the merits of the situation that meaning is at once imminent in the half-formed half-convinced situations in which externals are the only universals.

The growth of artistic situation in *Pañcatantra* and *The Canterbury Tales* suggests a growth along the differential and varying lines. For example, in *Pañcatantra* (Mitrabheda) the artistry generates the strength in the form of a universal condition of humanity in which every situation, every object and every event is absolutely capable of meeting a qualification for the enrichment of will, involvement and comprehension of the world at large. On the other hand, in Knight's Tale, the construct and figures both enter into an irreversible situation from where they cannot return, therefore, the imagination of character is always at odds with pursuit of the same characters.

## III

Warmth is a situation of involvement in which the object, the subject and the event are in mutual harmony, and, therefore, the situation is close to extending a concern for each and every moment. The motive of subject is to encourage the perception of reason through a proper set of correlatives, and, for this reason, sometimes, so much is engrossed into the object that it becomes difficult to say if the subject is subject or subject is object. Warmth is a necessary condition of the emergence and the birth of human consciousness because of the fact that humanity is reciprocal to the grasp of a method in the objects and this method is brought about by the worldly effect that warmth achieves and creates. So, for us one of the abstruse situations of understanding the warmth is to see it as a culmination of the humanity. On the whole, we can understand that warmth is an associated effect of proposing and balancing the perfect, absolute, total and harmoniums creation of the human experience.

## IV

In *Pañcatantra* and *The Canterbury Tales*, the ideals of warmth are expressed through strength and richness provided to it by the universal terms of human behaviour.

In *Pañcatantra*, warmth comes to be presented through two key situations. In the first place, the character becomes greatly expanded and enriched so as to include each and everybody, and, second, the willingness to impart a system of faith and contention to each and everybody is also remarkably helpful in determining the strength of the person. A character in *Pañcatantra* is not only curious about his self and his destiny but he is also greatly convinced in terms and prospects in the scheme of destiny and for this reason he always sees his fellow beings with confidence, concern and sympathy. We can admit the fact that the context that determines the object and the subject is itself progressive in nature because of this fact, it does not leave any room for suspicion and doubt:

> भो: शङ्कुकर्ण, स्वामी तावत्पथ्यं विना क्षुधया परिपीड्यते । स्वाम्यभावादस्माकमपि ध्रुवं विनाश एव । ततो वाक्यं कित्स्वाम्यर्थे वदिष्यामि। तच्छ्रयताम् । शङ्कुकर्ण आह – 'भो:, शीघ्रं निवेद्यताम्, येन ते वचन शीघ्रं निर्विकल्पं करोमि । अपरं स्वामिनो हिते कृते मया सुकृतशतं कृतं भविष्यति ।' अथ चतुरक आह – 'भो भद्र, आत्मशरीरं द्विगुणलाभेन स्वामिने प्रयच्छ, येन ते द्विगुणं शरीरं भवति, स्वामिन: पुन: प्राणयात्रा भवति ।
>
> *bhoḥ śaṅkukarṇa, svāmī tāvatpathyaṁ vina kṣudhayā paripīḍyate*। *svāmyabhāvādasmākamapi dhruvaṁ vināśa eva*। *tato vākyaṁ kitsvāmyarthe vadiṣyāmi* । *tacchrayatām* । *śaṅkukarṇa āha – 'bhoḥ, śīghraṁ nivedyatām, yena te vacana śīghraṁ nirvikalpaṁ karomi* । *aparaṁ svāmino hite kr̥te mayā sukr̥taśataṁ kr̥taṁ bhaviṣyati* ।' *atha caturaka āha – 'bho bhadra, ātmaśarīraṁ dviguṇalābhena svāmine prayaccha, yena te dviguṇaṁ śarīraṁ bhavati, svāminaḥ punaḥ prāṇayātrā bhavati*।
> – *Pañcatantra*, Mitrabheda, p. 164

The situation presented by Viṣṇuśarmā in this episode defines the very concept of warmth. In this, the lion, Vajradaṁṣṭra and its attendants Caturaka and Kravyamukha express their willingness to conceive the formation of content in which the inward and outward selves become precisely clear. Vajradaṁṣṭra transforms himself into the mercy holder by receiving the spirit of progression and growth inspiring the baby camel to become familiar with the newly-found generosity, and, therefore, he grows and enriches. The lion is brought to the condition of rather typical situation in which he could reinvent his determination to resolve a crisis in generosity. He unfolds and opens an equation and through which he sums up the figure in the manner of square. This is to say that the lion is irresolvable in the present circumstances, where he is the best among the unequals. The point to be understood is how the lion arranges and manages to consolidate the abstraction on the one hand, and incoherence on the other. The primary reason seems to be the symbolic function assigned to each of the characters in the present situation. A jackal, a fox and the baby camel come up with strange persuasive interests. In the jackal, greed is remarkable in the fox, the cunningness is absolute and in the baby camel insecurity is primary. It is now well open that the formal nature and subjective situation bring about a harmony of the situations therefore each is quite happy in a form and in a manner in which one assumes oneself. The authority of the lion is perfected to such an extent that he becomes a correlative of attitude that stands between himself and the baby camel, and, in that way, prefixes a complete disintegration of pride and ego.

In the Knight's Tale, the characters anticipate a rather disinterested and disengaged point of view, therefore, their concern with situation is mounted a material structure. The Knight, Arcite and Palamon, and also Emily, disengaged in such a way that the objectivity of the situation is lost. The reason behind this is that the interrelationship of one character with other and other with another is such that no one is in a position to find any ethical, religious or cultural code for oneself.

There is a difference only in relation to their engagement in crisis-oriented situations like love, hate, pride, lust, desire and praise, otherwise there is no involvement as such. A question may be asked at this stage as to how the organic and emotive foundations of life sustain or prolong in the midst of crisis-oriented structures. There are two different ways in which we can approach an answer to this question. In the first place, it must be understood that preliminary debate of an individual with the personal and private circumstances does not conduce to any formal meditation and comprehension. The intention to enrich oneself with a motivation to finally defeat the rise and growth of conscious pride is not very successful in respect of the scheme of characterization adopted by Western authors. It appears as if the individual is circumstantially and situationally misplaced, displaced or ill placed to handle the job of the fellow beings. His native temperament and the cultural tradition that he has inherited may be in opposition to the contentions he is inculcating for the sake of mature performance in the life.

In *The Canterbury Tales*, the formal aspect of humanity is not only typical but deeply material and worldly therefore the consumption of desire is in the action of the motive pursued by the characters. The Knight is a worldly wise man, and, for that matter, he gives an acceptance to the freedom of desire hence brings Emily to the context of love and romance. In Palamon and Arcite this play of desire encourages the individual to remain stuck to the worldly constraints yet this is not enough to substantially prove the point that the Knight is committed to any form and function of the absolute. He is merely engaged with the predominance of a rather limited expression of humanity. The wisdom and virtue of a character indicate its own suitability to a formal process, like, for example, he could look at a person and could ask him of his well-being, and beyond that the concern is left to the incoming situation. This is to say that the object–subject relationship is formalized only on those occasions in which the person attends to the peripheral association. For example, look at the following:

> *'Suster,' quod he, 'this is my fulle assent,*
> *With al thavys heer of my parlement,*
> *That gentil Palamon, your owne Knight,*
> *That serveth you with wille, herte, and might,*
> *And ever hath doon, sin that ye first him knewe,*
> *That ye shul, of your grace, up-on him rewe,*
> *And taken him for housbonde and for lord:*
> *Leen me your hond, for this is our accord.*
> *Lat see now of your wommanly pitee.*
> *He is a kinges brother sone, pardee;*
> *And, though he were a povre bacheler,*
> *Sin he hath served yow so many a yeer,*
> *And had for yow so greet adversitee,*
> *It moste been considered, leveth me;*
> *For gentil mercy oghte to passen right.'*
> – Chaucer 1958: 87

Here we can understand that the attitude of the Knight is harmoniously in correspondence with those of his sister Emily, and, for that matter, both have an agreement to put up a resolved condition for an activity in the growth of life. The Knight sanctions an idea for the marriage of Emily, for that matter, he also upgrades him to achieve a truthful model of his own being. On the other side of equation, stands Emily who puts a view so as to streamline stray experiences and expressions, and finally succeeds in this figural and material business of life. We can see that the Knight is enabled on account of an experience and Emily is enriched on account of expression and finally succeeds in this figural and material business of life. The function of experience is to assure the formation of logical distance between the presentation of the situation and reception of the same situation. The presentation itself is never allowed to meet the required standard of committed morality for this reason. The Knight has to come out with a promise to marry Emily to a person of her choice. It is important to know that Emily has an independent existence that is why Emily appears in the manner of assertive situation. The Knight, on the other hand, becomes befitting symbol of pride, honour and trust. The concern of the Knight for his sister operates in the manner of rightful and genuine identification of a brother's emotions for his sister yet he becomes fully convincing and authentic in maintaining a distance from the actual conduct and actual concern. The scale of expression of concern is purely local and ordinary.

The application of warmth to the human affairs and business of the life must be understood through the terms of comprehension that one is likely to meditate. Silence, patience, endurance, actual wisdom and curiosity for advancement and progress in the life of anybody are concerned with his zeal and enthusiasm for life. In this context, the idea contained in *Pañcatantra* appears to be a prescription for being complete, absolute and perfect. Viṣṇuśarmā comes out with an idea that life is a series of conclusion and resolutions, if the different actors are merely in a position to put up a face before the concrete models.

कुलीरकस्तच्छ्रुत्वा प्राह – 'माम, किं तद्वैराग्यकारणम् ।' स प्राह – 'वत्स, अहमस्मिन्सरसि जातो वृद्धिं गतश्च । तन्मयैतच्छ्रुतं यद्द्वादशवार्षिक्यनावृष्टिः सम्पद्यते लग्ना ।' कुलीरक आह – 'कस्मातच्छ्रुतम् ।' वक आह – दैवज्ञमुखात् एष शनैश्चरो हि रोहिणीशकटं भित्त्वा भौमं शुक्रं च प्रयास्यति ।

*kulīrakastacchrutvā prāha – 'māma, kiṁ tadvairāgyakāraṇam ।' sa prāha*

> – *'vatsa, ahamasminsarasi jāto vr̥ddhiṁ gataśca । tanmayaitacchrutaṁ yaddvādaśavārṣikyanāvr̥ṣṭiḥ sampadyate lagnā ।' kulīraka āha kasmātacchrutam । vaka āha – daivajñamukhāt eṣa śanaiścaro hi rohiṇīśakataṁ bhittvā bhaumaṁ śukraṁ ca prayāsyati ।*
>
> – *Pañcatantra*, Mitrabheda, p. 92

In this, there is confrontation between the Cancer and the Swan and the whole matter has been presented in such a way that truth appears to be looming large on both the sides. Cancer inquires the Swan about legitimacy of life prospects. In view of the sorrow of the Cancer, the Swan gently shows his inability to resolve the crisis brought about by his old age. It is understood here that the life is a presentation of milder attitudes even if the attending crisis appears to be great. There is no food, the Swan is not in a position to eat anything and it is old. These three facts make the point clear that presentation of the opportunities is unequal and varies from point to point. The deprivation is a consequence consequently the characters suffer on account of this. On the other side of his face, the Swan is in a position to conduct himself to the business of unsettling the established codes. The Cancer offers himself to an attitude of generosity and in this way tries to level the field. The effective position of these two animals is precisely to give an occasion of reasonable understanding, hence we can see that the Cancer turns the external situations into the frustration and despair since he has not been able to procure the food. This is an important development in the enrichment of greater perception of warmth. These creatures are involved in conduct of the occasion so as to get the opportunity of putting up the best of themselves, the Cancer with his innocence and the Swan with his selfishness and cunningness come to oppose as well as motivate each other. As characters, they can be said to have found ethical attitude of participation in which laws of morality and generosity are the primary points of attention. In that way we can say that the inner strength grants them an opportunity to express the largest possible freedom through wisdom, innovation and prudence.

The corresponding situation in the Knight's Tale neither is promising nor encouraging. Knight, Emily, Arcite and Palamon, though slightly elevated yet merely defied, bring up chaotic and anarchical.

The Knight's is a vague adjustment in a rather hopeless world of make and believe. He tries to substantiate the various situations of reality and unreality with zeal and enthusiasm. Emily, on other hand, sees the world as a motive of fulfilment of the basic instincts and desire, and, therefore, she falls in love immediately at the first sight with two Knights Palamon and Arcite. This situation makes it clear that the purpose of attending to the merit of choice and immediately catching the sight of the choice is to advance a personal cause for the sake of efficient working of the relations. It is not that Chaucer views the native condition of life to be not conducive for the temperament to refine rather he firmly believes in explaining the realistic situation attending the life. The method of articulating a concern for presentation is not as narrow as it comes to be in the Knight's Tale between the glories of war and conquests. In the gentle and soothing emotion of love, the choice is wide open. One can either transmute victory into love or despise, the love by calling it meek, subdued and submissive. In the Knight's Tale, one learns that the necessity of assertion and exposition, and, for that matter, the Knight succumbs to his sister's advances towards her lovers. The basic proposition that one learns and understands is that of extreme concentration and condensation of the characters which are virtually placed upon these enterprises. The growth and development of an extreme individual is perhaps at the bottom of European narrative tradition. John Bunyan, for example, in *The Pilgrim's Progress* makes mention of the following:

> Obstinate: What are the things you seek, since you leave all the world to find them?"
>
> Christian: "I seek an 'inheritance, incorruptible, undefiled, and that fadeth not away,' [1 Peter 1:4] and it is laid up in Heaven, and fast there, to be bestowed at the time appointed on them that diligently seek it. Read it so, if you will, in my book.
>
> Obstinate: "Tush," said Obstinate, "away with your book; will you go back with us or not?"
>
> Christian: "No, not I" said the other, "because I have laid my hand to the plaw" (Luke 9:62).

> Obstinate: "Come, then, neighbour Pliable, let us turn again, and go home without him; there is a company of these crazed-headed coxcombs, that when they take a fancy by the end are wiser in their own eyes than seven men that can render a reason." (Proverbs 26:16).
>
> – Bunyan 1969: 20

The emphasis is precisely on how to emerge from a situation in which rage and sin have become a sign of enragement and annihilation, and, obviously, compulsions at work generate the conditionality for destruction. In John Bunyan's *The Pilgrim's Progress*, Christian finds himself in only reducing terms. There would be no place for men to live in and surprisingly, Christian decides in favour of approaching the sanctity of the terms, therefore, he excludes himself from the occasion. In *The Pilgrim's Progress* and Knight's Tale one sees how eminence of form presupposes growth of the character. In Knight's Tale, the rage in love and in *The Pilgrim's Progress*, it is rage in sin that forestall the growth of a growing character. The idea of displeasing and dislocating the character at the site of imminent danger is supposed to be at the heart of Western narrative tradition, yet the magnitude and intensity of this problem varies from narrative to narrative and some historical determinants are also become unquestionably sole components of the situation.

In Indian and European narratives, the concern of the character for himself, his other selves, his larger selves and his universal selves constitutes perception through which the author intends the complete transformation of an individual into action so as to determine the content for such an exclusive excellence. The authors of the narrative in both the traditions uphold the validity of discretion, wisdom, prudence and withhold the formal methods and approach the signification of the whole process. In *Pañcatantra*, for example, we can see that the characters go on manifesting a proper attitude in being real, being appropriate and also being valid for the terms of comprehension that they came to enjoy with their fellow beings. These are not led away by the momentary and temporary glimpses of illusory forms that make the external of substances visible in instinct. The material forms do not invent the convergence of consciousness and hence the characters are generally in a position to retain concrete form in which they had their creation.

The origin of such a concern could be very well seen and understood in visible distinction that an action tends to offer to the magnitude of commitment. There could be as many varieties of the formation of an attitude of motive in the action and character yet the primary concern is just to settle its trait as random quotient. In the Knight's Tale, the Knight promises the virtue and accords a credit to this virtue by motivating an equal amount of love through a separation of individual from his ego, for this, he has to slightly acquire motive and for the purpose he destroys the presentation of ego in the normal facets of conscience hence we are in a position to see Theseus, Palamon, Emily and Arcite as having an approval through the functionality of meaningful situations (Theseus as the father sanctioning the prosperity of Arcite and Palamon).

*And either syde y-lyk, as otheres brother;*
*And yaf hem yiftes after hir degree,*
*And fully heeld a feste dayes three,*
*And conveyed the kinges worthily,*
*Out of his toun a Iournee largely.*
*And hoom wente every man the righte way.*
*Ther was namore, but 'far wel, have good day!'*
*Of this bataille I wol namore endyte,*
*But speke of Palamon and of Arcite.*

– Chaucer 1958: 78

To judge the situation, one can easily understand the fair play of motives in the development and commencement of love. The advancement of situation, the choice of goodwill, generosity (concern), care and at the extreme end of nobility are wisdom and virtue. When one is well one thinks well and when one considers the whole humanity to be an extension of the general motives presented in one's thought and manner of thinking, one admits a concern of equality for everybody. The spirit of composing a mark of attention exposes and the tenure of exposition validates the function of conviction. This necessity could be seen to be another important feature in the conduct of humanity in whatever form it comes to be in the Western narratives. For example, at the very beginning of *The Decameron*, Boccaccio (1951: 4) states quite convincingly:

> This horrid beginning will be to you even such as to Wayfarers is a steep and rugged mountain, beyond which stretches a plain most fair and delectable, which the toil of the ascent and descent does but serve to render more agreeable to them; for, as the last degree of joy brings with it sorrow; so misery has ever its sequel of happiness.

The strength of forming cohesion through a deeper involvement into the affair of the man has been conclusively proved through the varieties of enactments. For example, the author considers the terms of applicability of one's wishes through frank, clear, consolidated and concentrated utterances. This is enough to show how an individual could be moved and cycled so as to distinctly credit himself in the matters of welfare and progress. In the Knight's Tale, one has the opportunities to find out how the mind of men must work to resolve an imposition of the largest possible comprehension. That is perhaps the best thing that anybody can do at any event of time.

In this way, we are invited to attend the situation inhering upon Viṣṇuśarmā's *Pañcatantra* and Chaucer's the Knight's Tale where the warmth of a person or an application of one's interest in other, so as to elevate and ennoble the both, becomes a primary ground of comprehension, evaluation and analysis. The basic qualities of situation are helping, solving, dissolving, resolving, creating, building and justifying how individual could stand in relation to each other and one another.

## IV

Involvement is a sense of recognition in which the basis of recognition is conformity to meaning that comes through the disposition of a being. The basic cause of involvement is goodness of feeling, applicability of once own intention in relation to idea, attitudes (activities) and concern in involvement. Two situations are considered to be primarily responsible. In the first place, the person is invited to frankly express himself. His disposition is so well elevated and motivated that he always looks for equivalent concern. Second, the individual feels the necessity of proving the worth of his own position through a remarkable set of associative elements. These two necessary points of determination of the birth of individual decide the extent to which the class of involvement would be obtained. In that way we can understand as to how the matter of cohesion, synthesis, association, correlation and concomitant is strongly presented.

In *Pañcatantra* and *The Canterbury Tales*, the idea of recreation of an object into a form, a subject, or a subject into an event, or even otherwise the object and the subject into resolution precisely tell us about the fundamental grounds of humanity. The involvement appears in object's assurance to the immediate situations for the discovery of an ideal, homogeneous and suitable atmosphere. This is to say that different situations in *Pañcatantra* bring about a commitment for approval and change, similarly, in *The Canterbury Tales* involvement is a condition for having an entrance into the wider facets of humanity. It is to be seen and understood that the humanity is largest possible facet of the growth of sensibility of either the object or the subject in such a way that the meaning of concern is understood by everybody. The chief function of humanity is to restore the dignity of the situation of event which proposes an appropriate and valid code of action. In *Pañcatantra*, the aspect of involvement brings up a complete transformation of an individual into another individual and an action into another event and an event into another action for the sake of many-sided growth and development of personality. In other words, we can say that the object and the subject both are capable of multiple appearances and multiple incarnations. Look at the following for example:

> पिंगलक आह – 'यद्येवं तर्ह्यमात्यपदेऽध्यारोपितस्त्वम्। अद्यप्रभृति प्रसादनिग्रहादिकं त्वयैव कार्यमिति निचयः ।'
>
> अथ दमनकः सत्वरं गत्वा साक्षेपं तमिदमाह – 'ऐह्येहीतो दुष्टवृषभ! स्वामी पिंगलकस्त्वामाकारयति । किं निःशटो भूत्वा मुहुर्मुहुर्नदसि वृथा' इति ।

तच्छ्रुत्वा सजीवकोऽब्रवीत् - 'भद्र, कोऽयं पिंगलक:'। दमनक आह - 'किं स्वामिनं पिंगलकमपि न जानासि । तत्क्षणप्रतिपालय । फलेनैव ज्ञास्यसि । नन्वयं सर्वमृगपरिवृतो वटतले स्वामी पिंगलकनामा सिंहस्तिष्ठति ।' तच्छ्रुत्वा गतायुषमिवात्मानं मन्यमान: सजीवक: परं विषादमगमत् । आह च - 'भद्र, भवान् साधुसमाचारो वचनपटुच दृश्यते । तद्यदि मामवश्यं तत्र नयसि तदभयप्रदानेन स्वामिन: सकाशात् प्रसाद: कारियतव्य: । दमनक आह - भो:, सत्यमभिहितं भवता ।

*piṅgalaka āha – 'ydyevaṁ tarhyamātyapade 'dhyāropitastvam । adyaprabhṛti prasādanigrahādikaṁ tvayaiva kāryamiti nicayaḥ ।'*

*atha damanakaḥ satvaraṁ gatvā sākṣepaṁ tamidamāha – 'ehyehīto duṣṭavṛṣabha! svāmī piṅgalakastvāmākārayati । kiṁ niḥśaṭo bhūtvā muhurmuhurnadasi vṛthā' iti । tacchrutvā sajīvako 'bravīt – 'bhadra, ko 'yaṁ piṅgalakaḥ' । damanaka āha – 'kiṁ svāminaṁ piṅgalakamapi na jānāsi । tatkṣaṇapratipālaya । phalenaiva jñāsyasi । nanvayaṁ sarvamṛgaparivṛto vaṭatale svāmī piṅgalakanāmā siṁhastiṣṭhati ।' tacchrutvā gatāyuṣamivātmānaṁ manyamānaḥ sajīvakaḥ paraṁ viṣādamagamat । āha ca – 'bhadra, bhavān sādhusamācāro vacanapaṭuca dṛśyate । tadyadi māmavaśyaṁ tatra nayasi tadabhayapradānena svāminaḥ sakāśāt prasādaḥ kāriyatavyaḥ । damanaka āha – bhoḥ, satyamabhihitaṁ bhavatā ।* – *Pañcatantra*, Mitrabheda, p. 41

In this episode, we can say that Piṅgalaka, the lion, proposes manifold stretch of his personality. In the first place, he is a lion; second, he is the king; third, he is universal; and fourth, he is truth. In order to measure himself as a symbol in each of these he invites Damanaka to render himself into an object of correlation and synthesis hence Damanaka becomes a method through which Piṅgalaka issues himself in the midst of overwhelming odds. It means that the novelty of character is not only confined or limited to immediate reflections or rather it has a truthful form. Piṅgalaka is a king and he must assert without succumbing to the monumental pressure from the external world, therefore, Piṅgalaka has the ability to withstand the harror of appearance mounted as threat through Sañjīvaka, the ox.

The style of enabling the unforeseen to become the concept of a situation is purely understood by Piṅgalaka. Between Piṅgalaka and Sañjīvaka, there is a remote and distant bond of affection and warmth because neither Piṅgalaka nor Sañjīvaka antidates the other. The virtue of one, is, in fact, a manifestation of the faith one has in prospering the cause of one's sympathy. We understand that Piṅgalaka does not mount attack on Sañjīvaka rather he goes on with reconciliation. There is no horror as such, therefore, there is only content of horrors that comes for passing attention and is so well understood that Sañjīvaka or Piṅgalaka is in a position to exchange the codes of identities – the king and the subject, and the subject and the king. This manner of interposing an attitudinal involvement is the basic question that has been asked in *Pañcatantra* and repeatedly Viṣṇuśarmā tries to put forth convincing answer by building up the situation. In an episode dealing with the Stork and different creature living in a pond, the idea of involvement is grand and universal:

> अथ ते सर्वे भयत्रस्तमनसो मत्स्यकच्छपप्रभृतयस्तमभ्युपेत्य पप्रच्छुः – 'माम, अस्ति कचि दुपायो येनास्माकं रक्षा भवति । बक आह – 'अस्त्यस्य जलाशयस्य नातिदूरे प्रभूतजलसनाथं सरः पद्मिनीखण्डमण्डितं यच्चतुर्विंशत्यपि वर्षाणामवृष्टया न शोषमेष्यति । तद्यदि मम पृष्ठं कचिदारोहति तदहं तं तत्र नयामि ।' अथ ते तत्र विश्वासमापन्नाः 'तात, मातुल, भ्रातः' इति ब्रुवाणाः 'अहं पूर्वमहं पूर्वम्' इति समन्तात्परितस्थुः । सोऽपि दुष्टाशयः क्रमेण तान्पृष्ठ आरोप्य जलाशयस्य नातिदूरे शिलां समासाद्य तस्यामाक्षिप्य स्वेच्छया भक्षयित्वा भूयोऽपि जलाशयं समासाद्य जलचराणां मिथ्यावार्तासन्देशकैर्मनांसि राज्यन्नित्यमेवाहारवृत्तिमकरोत्। अन्यस्मिन्दिने च कुलीरकेणोक्तः 'माम, मया सह ते प्रथमः स्नेहसम्भाषः सजतः। तत्कि मां परित्यज्यान्यान्नयसि । तस्मादद्य मे प्राणत्राणं कुरु ।' तदाकर्ण्य सोऽपि दुष्टाशयचिन्ततवान् – 'निर्विण्णोऽहं मत्स्यमांसादनेन तदद्यैनं कुलीरकं व्य जनस्थाने करोमि ।' इति विचिन्त्य तं पृष्टे समारोप्य तां वध्यशिलामुद्दिश्य प्रस्थितः । कुलीरकोऽपि दूरादेवास्थिपर्वतं शिलाश्रयमवलोक्य मत्स्यास्थीनि परिज्ञाय तमपृच्छत् – 'माम, कियद्दूरे स जलाशयः मदीयभारेणातिश्रान्तस्त्वम् । तत्कथय ।'

> *atha te serve bhayatrastamanaso matsyakacchapaprabhṛtayastamabhyupetya papracchuḥ – 'māma, asti kaci dupāyo yenāsmākaṁ rakṣā bhavati* ǀ *baka āha – 'astyasya jalāśayasya nātidūre prabhūtajalasanāthaṁ saraḥ padminīkhaṇḍamaṇḍitaṁ yaccaturviṁśatyapi varṣāṇāmavṛṣṭayā na śoṣameṣyati* ǀ *tadyadi mama pṛṣṭhaṁ kacidārohati tadahaṁ taṁ tatra nayāmi* ǀ*' atha te tatra viśvāsamāpannāḥ 'tāta, mātula, bhrātaḥ' iti bruvāṇāḥ 'ahaṁ pūrvamahaṁ pūrvam' iti samantātparitasthuḥ* ǀ *so 'pi duṣṭāśayaḥ krameṇa tānpṛṣṭha āropya jalāśayasya nātidūre śilāṁ samāsādya tasyāmākṣipya svecchayā bhakṣayitvā bhūyo 'pi*

> *jalāśayaṁ samāsādya jalacarāṇāṁ mithyāvārtāsandeśakairmanāṁsi rājyannityamevāhāravṛttimakarot* | *anyasmindine ca kulīrakeṇoktaḥ 'māma, mayā saha te prathamaḥ snehasambhāṣaḥ sajataḥ* | *tatki māṁ parityajyānyānnayasi* | *tasmādadya me prāṇatrāṇaṁ kuru* |' *tadākarṇya so 'pi duṣṭāśayacintatavān – 'nirviṇṇo 'haṁ matsyamāṁsādanena tadadyainaṁ kulīrakaṁ vya janasthāne karomi* |' *iti vicintya taṁ pṛṣṭe samāropya tāṁ vadhyaśilāmuddiśya prasthitaḥ* | *kulīrako 'pi dūrādevāsthiparvataṁ śilāśrayamavalokya matsyāsthīni parijñāya tamapṛcchat – 'māma, kiyaddūre sa jalāśayaḥ madīyabhāreṇātiśrānt-stvam* | *tatkathayah* |' – *Pañcatantra*, Mitrabheda, p. 110

The Stork, despite being an enemy, is considering the revival of uniform equality of concern, through which he could have the idea and attitude. The creatures in the pond are similarly zeal-oriented and they intend prosperity through mutual compatibility. These two are only the stages in growth of perceptible form and therefore they consider him to be a model through which they can transmute themselves. This progress that creatures are contemplating and meditating is supposed to be activated through the marginal terms and that is why this approach between stork and the other creatures of pond. There is an alliance of brevity with seriousness everybody feels, acts, creates, and harmonizes the natural and primary forms of concept, and, for that matter, the Stork conceives cruelty as a method to fulfil a mission of rage and the creature themselves approach the warmth and goodwill for each and everybody. This situation is not only unique but also in the tradition of fair narratives.

To match the condition to equal the enterprise by putting up an antithesis, a larger equivalent appears in the form of Cancer. While we assess the relative position of the Stork and the Cancer in terms of their deceit and benevolence, we can immediately presume that there is an interchange and exchange of conjunctions; the Stork stands as a demotivated and insincere figure and a form of faithlessness. His presumption and imagination do not make him fit to be an equal partner, therefore, he dislocates himself and distinguishes himself by comprehending absolutely dysfunctional model in that he kills the fellow creatures; killing is an act of surprise and wonder at that because it degenerates the native perception and disorients the model of experience. Cancer on the other hand serves his concrete embodiment and for that, goes on to save him by merely apprehending the imbalance of cause and effect. "That whether of yow bothe that hath might. . . . Him shal I yeve Emelya to wyve" (Chaucer 1958: 117). Chaucer takes different positions with regard to the working of the whole structure. Involvement is an act of one's ability to withstand the rise and fall of fortune in such a way that the fortune is immediately felt to be one's own condition of existence to come to terms with the changing circumstances of the life. In the Knight's Tales, the attitude of Theseus (the Knight) in placing himself in all the extraordinary ups and downs and thereby qualifying himself in the model-oriented presentation is extraordinary. For example, in a situation in which he is supposed to come out with qualified terms for his daughter, he adjudicates by approving a comprehensive option which the marriage of Emily would be not by choice but by trial of wisdom, might and intellect. Here we can understand that Knight for an effective taste of wisdom. In other words, we can say that he rejects the immediate opportunity and goes with the universal form obtained in the conduct of terms. We may think of saying that the Knight synthesizes the conjunctions for a proper and fair internalization of upcoming ideas.

The conditions that go on to make involvement a necessary principle are as comprehensive as an ability to immediately modify the speech by inverting necessary illusions. It means that those who involve themselves to explicate various terms for humanity are also those who concretize the strength of illusion as being models of reality, recognization, consideration, conformation and consolidation. Involvement, is, in fact, a correlation that each figure is become awareness in the present. For example, look at the following:

> तच्च दृष्ट्वा सहसैव कश्चिच्चौरश्चिन्तितवान् – 'अहमस्य ब्राह्मणस्य गोयुगमिदमपहरिष्यामि, इति निश्चित्य निशायां बन्धनपाशं गृहीत्वा, यावत्प्रस्थितस्तावदर्धमार्गे प्रविरलतीक्ष्णदन्तपंक्ति स्नातनासावंशः, प्रकटरक्तान्तनयनः उपचितस्नायुसन्तततनतगात्रः शुष्ककपोलः सुहुतहुतवहपिंगलश्मश्रुकेशशरीरः कश्चिद् दृष्टः। दृष्ट्वा च तं तीव्रभयस्तोऽपि चौराऽब्रवीत् – 'को भवान्' इति । स आह –

'सत्यवचनोऽहं ब्रह्मराक्षसः । भवानप्यात्मानं निवेदयतु ।' सोऽब्रवीत् – 'अहं क्रूरकर्मा चौरो दरिद्रब्राह्मणस्य गोयुगं हर्तुं प्रस्थितोऽस्मि।' अथ जातप्रत्ययो राक्षसोऽब्रवीत् – भद्र! षष्ठाह्नकालिकोऽहम् ।' अतस्तमेव ब्राह्मणमद्य भक्षयिष्यामि; तत्सुन्दरमिदम्, एककार्यावेवावाम् ।' अथ तौ तत्र गत्वैकान्ते कालमन्वेषयन्तौ स्थितौ ।

*tacca dṛṣṭvā sahasaiva kaciccauracintitavān – 'ahamasya brāhmaṇasya goyugamidamapahariṣyāmi, iti nicitya niśāyāṁ bandhanapāśaṁ gṛhītvā, yāvatprasthitastāvadardhamārge praviralatīkṣṇadantapaṅkti srātanāsāvaṁśaḥ, prakaṭaraktāntanayanaḥ upacitasnāyusantata-natagātraḥ śuṣkakapolaḥ suhutahutavahapiṅgalaśmaśrukeśaśarīraḥ kacid dṛṣṭaḥ | dṛṣṭvā ca taṁ tīvrabhyasto 'pi caurā 'bravīt – 'ko bhavān' iti | sa āha – 'satyavacano 'haṁ brahmarākṣasaḥ | bhavānapyātmānaṁ nivedayatu |' so 'bravīt – 'ahaṁ krūrakarmā cauro daridrabrāhmaṇasya goyugaṁ hartuṁ prasthio 'smi |' atha jātapratyayo rākṣaso 'bravīt – bhadra! ṣaṣṭhāhnakāliko 'ham |' atastameva brāhmaṇamadya bhakṣayiṣyāmi; tatsundaramidam, ekakāryāvevāyām |' atha tau tatra gatvaikānte kālamanveṣayantan sthitau |*

– *Pañcatantra*, Kākolūkīyam, p. 65

In this situation, a Demon and a thief are united for a common cause to commit a theft at the house of a brāhmaṇa, and that too of a cow and an ox. Both enter into a connivance thereby rectify the purpose of illusion and illusion itself being the fulfilment of some unfulfilled needs. In this enterprise, the Demon and the thief both are situated on scale of a commitment that disappears so as to make them constantly in search of a fine reality. The cow that is to be stolen is not a reality; it is only a purpose unto the actual situation; and these two agents who claim to be pursuing this, end up only with a sight of disappearance of the purported object. It can be seen that the object in the present context makes a challenge to the imagination of both the characters so as to embody them with a series of purposelessness. While considering this fact, one has to concede the point that the goal, the preference and the ambition of the characters are common in so far as they meet to enact their ideal attitude for the benefit of each other. Individualities of the characters provide them a method to revive their coherence. The Demon is invariably the assurance and that is undoubtedly Demon's projection and goodwill and by that standard they are united and brought together. When we speak of illusion as an important object of consideration, we mean, by that, a necessary dislocation of the present context. There are better ways to know how this function is obtained in *Pañcatantra* and *The Canterbury Tales*. The following characteristic could well be presumed to be underlined as basic assumptions of involvement in the making of humanity in these two great works of art. Involvement facilitates the process of coordination among individuals. For example, look at the following:

> *nought greveth us your glorie and your honour;*
> *But we biseken mercy and socour.*
> *Have mercy on our wo and our distresse.*
> *Some drope of pitee, thrugh thy gentillesse,*
> *Up-on us wrecched wommen lat thou falle.*
> *For certes, lord, ther nis noon of us alle.*
>
> – Chaucer 1958: 27

Involvement encourages the concern of opportunity to have in turn a concern for the collective growth and progress. For example, see the following:

> *Arcite is hurt as muche as he, or more.*
> *And with a sigh he seyde pitously:*
> *'The fresshe beautee sleeth me sodeynly*
> *Of hir that rometh in the yonder place;*
> *And, but I have hir mercy and hir grace,*
> *That I may seen hir ate leeste weye.*
> *I nam but deed; ther nis namore to seye.*
>
> – Ibid.: 33

Involvement handles the situation of extremity of violence of attitude in such a way that both the object and the subject are brought to a point of common concern. For example:

> *Love if thee list; for I love and ay shal;*
> *And soothly, leve brother, this is al.*
> *Here in this prisoun mote we endure,*
> *And everich of us take his aventure.*
>
> – Ibid.: 35, 325-28

Involvement, at the same time, infuses a model into an object so that both of these may appear in the form of an absolute where the error of abstraction is minimum. For example:

*May, with alle thy floures and thy grene,*
*Wel-come be thou, faire fresshe May,*
*I hope that I som grene gete may.*
*And from his courser, with a lusty herte,*
*In-to the grove ful hastily he sterte.*

– Ibid.: 44

Involvement also enriches the sanctity of organization thereby it reduces the chance of disunity and misrecognition. For example:

*And this day fifty wykes, fer ne ner,*
*Everich of yow shal bringe an hundred knightes,*
*Armed for listes up at alle rightes,*
*Al redy to darreyne hir by bataille.*
*And this bihote I yow, with-outen faille,*
*Up-on my trouthe, and as I am a knight,*
*That whether of yow bothe that hath might,*
*That is to seyn, that whether he or thou.*

– Ibid.: 53

In this way, we can understand that the involvement is a basic necessity in projecting the variant of enriched individuality to the external space and external world. In *Pañcatantra*, the meaning of involvement is extended to the generosity that definitely becomes a universal content than that the content which as in *The Canterbury Tales* could bring about. The involvement becomes specific to those who share the commonality of purpose, motives, ideas and attitudes.

## V

The idea of humanity in *Pañcatantra* and *The Canterbury Tales* could be worked out through four major structures of conceptualization – involvement, warmth, comprehension and familiarity. In each of these structures, the basic issue is that of an individual who tries to advance thorough it, in the midst of various problems of the life, universe and the world. Therefore, in *Pañcatantra* and *The Canterbury Tales*, the celebrated authors have tried to examine primary models that could be conceived in the manner of universality in an individual, the family, the society, the nation, and, for that matter, the whole world. The idea of an individual has been compulsive or assertive. This remains one of the major concerns of the authors to develop their concept of humanity. Viṣṇuśarmā and Chaucer both have presented a canonical view of the beings, and, for that matter, their understanding of the beings is remarkable. Viṣṇuśarmā understands the beings to be as essentially perfect although he could fall and he could raise himself from the ruins of failure in that way the degeneration of canonical structure in the beings always leads to building up of enriched version for the degenerate form. It is for this reason that Viṣṇuśarmā locates the primacy of individual in the internal structures and external correlatives and when the individual grows in the direction of both the internal and external universe, nature, space, it would become three primary determinants of an individual or a character that happens to be performing his role in the making of the narrative. This would lead us to some important questions like – Where does the individual stay? What does it mean to fall? Why does an individual rise to primacy of relations? Viṣṇuśarmā has nearly answered all these questions in that he makes an individual to be always cyclical, functional, reversible and non-linear in nature. The question now arises as to how Viṣṇuśarmā has selected the functional and structural strength of canonical and ritual forms. The answer to this question seems to be lying in the fact that the progress of life at large is determined on account of coherence, harmony and synthesis that it generates through a generative, notional, orderly and harmonious approach. It is left to the ability of the individual as to how he opens up the possibility of errors of opposition and rectification of prejudices in any compulsive or assertive event. The life is bound to either make an experience at large for all to either gather or close the possibility of an experience. In *Pañcatantra*, there is an opening of experience and closing of an experience through the strength assumed by the objects/forms/subjects at various positions and the circumstances.

The individuals/objects/subjects propose an opening for

themselves into the world that is swept by likes and dislikes, passions and distrusts, births and deaths. For an object to become a part of this, it is necessary that it should be fully in a position to conceptualize the committed binary oppositions (like/dislike, existence/annihilation and love/hate). It cannot be said that an individual object/form could be well prepared to explore the possibility of a meaning in particular circumstances. These could either be a formal association or definite repulsion from the circumstances at work. In *Pañcatantra,* we come across smooth variation between the various corners of the life. The characters like Sañjīvaka, Damanaka, Piṅgalaka, Gaṅgādutta, Kravyamukha, Caturaka, Dantila, Vajradaṁṣṭra, Candroba and Madolakata are precisely the example of near total presentation of conceptual schemes of life. There is a perfect embodiment of goodwill, goodness, generosity, sincerity and commitment. The precise structure that determines the concept of humanity is constantly in a state of interference formation. For this reason, the character that has wickedness in him is opened to preferences and changes. The exchange of passion with regard to intentional meaning is perhaps one of the greater achievements in defining the particular wisdom. Viṣṇuśarmā fixes his eyes on the exceptional relationship that any form enjoys with his external world, and, to this end, he always makes it imminent that goodness triumphs and evil is defeated by the merits of behaviour created by the forms in *Pañcatantra*. We are brought to recognition that the form under consideration is having an unusual grasp of experience, and, because of that he is allowed to decay or prosper on the whole. We can understand that comprehension on the part of an object of following an individual of fellow objects/individuals is generative of strength, order and harmony.

## VI

In *The Canterbury Tales* of Chaucer, the concept of humanity has slightly different focuses and terminologies. In this, Chaucer says that the empirical forms attending the life are not always direct, flat, smooth and penetrating, accordingly, one suffers from being brought to the extreme, and hence we are more prone to vices (lust, rage, betrayal, evil and the like). It is not that a characteral formation does not intend any goodness for him; rather he explicates himself in inversion and faces the consequences. To substantiate this, we can survey the careers of such characters as the Knight, Sumner and Doctor of Physic. We are nearer to this truth in each of these; the sanctity of truth is expelled through the repulsive intrusion of dysfunction into the schemes of life.

## VII

In the Knight's Tale, Chaucer does create the framework of relational or relative discourse in which a form or an object obtaining the space in action is made to initiate a close-ended response throughout his career. In this narrative, he expects characters to make out a temporary scheme for himself to bring about a necessary simplification of experience. Character is motivated only to continue a style of living, for that matter there is a hardly an obstruction or even an impasse in the progress of the character towards a point of consummation. It is understood that the style opted by the character to understand his own particular problem and circumstances does not qualify him to become worthy of an absolute form. In the actual reading of the text, terms and actual causes of event explicate necessary expectation, promise and fulfilment. It does not find any fulfilment as such through the expectation incorporated in ethical and normative structure of the events. Theseus promises to be an ideal form, yet there are obvious destructions because of which the character does not prosecute him to the resolution. The Knight is an ideal but crudeness of the basic instinct underlying filial obligations mars the prospect of composite conduction. Hence the idealism of the Knight is abstracted by decadent and enfeebled morale of his sister Emily. This narrative closes, opposes and finally repels ideals, which are circumstantially made strong enough to deform the practice of sanctity. Emily's degeneration in the face of imperfect and inordinate love is remarkably obvious in the scheme of things adopted by Chaucer. Therefore, he concludes that the narrative deals with an action having temporary fixation for each and everybody. The Knight is relieved of the burden of responsibility of his sister Emily who is now married to Arcite. Although there are confirmed situations of impasse in the narrative, we are led to believe that the structure of humanity is evident in involvement, commitment, sincerity and comprehension. These four major structures work them up through short and half-indicated meanings. It would mean that humanity is a matter of compulsion because the people are instinctively inclined to lust and rage. This compulsive form is evident through the inability of the character to perform a reversal of methods of applicability of experience.

## VIII

It is now possible to say with conviction that *Pañcatantra* and *The Canterbury Tales* formalize a definite pattern of humanity. In *Pañcatantra,* humanity is truth and sanctity that are approved on account of internal strength and external coherence built up by the different forms/objects/individuals/characters that happen to be in various schemes of the things of life. On that account, the idea of humanity is an absolute, obtained in one's ability to familiarize the experience of oneself with larger and greater experience of fellow beings. On the other hand, in the Knight's Tale, humanity is merely a ritualistic, ceremonial and prudential act that is created through a deprivation of decadent experience in the general motive of the objects/forms/characters/individuals. *Pañcatantra,* for this reason, is magnificent, absolute and total expression of grown-up beings, while *The Canterbury Tales* is only illusory, blatant and enraged, to say without any malice of the strength of those persons who are chaotic, irregular and fragmentary.

# 5

# Resolution and Convergence : II

## Jātakakathāvalī and The Pilgrim's Progress

*Jātakakathāvalī* and *The Pilgrim's Progress* both present a comprehensive view of life in such a way that the ideals for life become suggestive of truth, honesty, commitment, sincerity and involvement. The presentation of narratives is in the manner of a continuous chain of events and each event formally prepares a set of characters to construct a typical scheme for the growth and perpetuation of life. In the *Jātaka Tales*, idea of bringing an individual nearer to the actual experience is utmost, in which the actual conditions of life generally find there expression. This generation of events calls for strength in the individual and the strength prepares the individual to become a mark of excellence. There can be two ways to expedite the process of change of individual into his greater form. The Jātakas are precisely born out of this struggle of a man to universalize himself by priority that *bodhisattva* gives to the relational circumstances for his own existence to mark an interpretation and examination of the extent of sanctity. The strength of virtue is so well encoded in him that he strikes out whatever is an embodiment of evil. The function, for that matter, is to promote unity of visual and non-visual contents in such a way that the truth that we realize and the evil we come across are standing in opposition to each other. There could be the primary motive in supporting this contention in so far as the stretch of truth and extent of evil are infinite and eternal. Truth does not prohibit the development of conscious or unconscious being. On the other hand, evil effectively restrains the mode and medium of expression and in that context the purity of truth must be an occasion for the complete transformation of being. For that matter, evil is obviously an imposition that cannot be called upon to sustain any condition of any wholesome category found within the consciousness of living beings. The Jātakas are exclusive and effective assertion of this situation. Construction of an evil and eradication of an evil both require magnitude and proportion since both are visible and real. It would be better to call the whole situation a purpose and an ambition allowing up gradation of the length of experience that is constantly changing. There may be certainty with regard to the lengthened form of imposition and constraint which come up for our persual yet the individual completes a series of curious acceptances of each such form and manners obviously. It would mean that in Jātakas, the narratives begin with a continuity of prosecution of real and actual along with two different shapes and vision. In the first place, we can have reception of a compulsion on the negative side of an appearance and here the individual forms do not acquire or even gather any strength whatsoever of structure of the regular form that is appearing before his eyes. For this reason, individual is misplaced, displaced and greatly moved away from the centre of causative perception hence we have evil in the life. The question arises as to how and why the effect of evil is not good and always bad? This interpretation of a sound factual judgement, outlined above, will have its roots in the external materialistic system and internal absolute of truth in the form of a soul. The inward contents are primarily real hence they align themselves with equally real forms outside. In the case of evil, realistic framework of the contents hardly succeed in composing the differential value of the external world resorting into separation of absolute and the reversible content form to obtain in the external constrained process. The worth of this idea is to promote necessity and encourage awareness in organization of the virtue as a principle of life. The motive of the analysis would show that the habit to call good as virtuous and bad as evil results from a predisposed movement of the equivalent from within either the object or the subject, and the individual has to perceive correlation between reality and the expression of reality or, in other words, between realizable false and extra-realizable false. It would then be a matter of exposing an expanding category to accomplish an equal participation in both. At once, the exclusion of evil and inclusion of virtue are a simultaneous process. Hence the structure of the form responds to both. Jātakas have shown with greater maturity how evil and virtue move in a cyclical form in which the strength of virtue is always in excess of that of evil. Of evil and virtue, virtue has a configuration in which structure is synthesized in the functional contents hence it opens up genuine possibility to complete the motive that it intends to create or bring about. It is to be taken as a form of assurance as to how the progress of virtue marks rise in the concentration of the rightful expression. External material system brings about decline in the strength of concentration and leads to decay in the organization of will and enthusiasm. Strength of will is to create a method of preparation for right and just commitment and the necessity for exposing the commitment is rightly made for the sake of an extensive formation of prohibitory attitude. Perception of evil is an act of commitment generated in the sanctity and identity of baser instincts, for this reason, in the case of evil there is no continuity in evolution. An experience generally evolves and receives an addition of content through both multiplication and conjunction; this is the largest possible extent through which we can think of exposing the Jātaka Tales to this conceptual construction of good and evil.

## II

The structure of the Jātakas is very comprehensive, broad, vast and penetrating in nature. Each of the Jātakas is in the form of a sermon delivered by one of the disciples of the Buddha. Consequently each narrative episode acquires the name of the Buddha's disciple concerned, since the narrative is in the form of a sermon; it is both implosive and persuasive. Reaction presented by this opposition between good and evil forms the basis of the groundwork of plot. In the Jātaka narratives, the main hero of the whole situation is *bodhisattva* himself, who happens to be embodying the spirit of God in himself and is quite capable of uprooting the cause of any evil so much so that he understands this truthful situation in which the experience of a person suggests the creation of meaning in every conceivable formation of goodness with a view to oppose badness. It would mean that the native form of truth has sufficient strength and power to determine its expression through many shades of situation in the terms of subjectivity where time enters into the formation as a mark of decay. Therefore, truth will have the opportunity to associate with the larger form of ideal experience. Decadent time connects the fragmentation and ruin together hence it also builds up hopelessness as a term of expression. The pragmatic function of any such experience is still not known. For this reason the model to carry subsequent evil will have the same authority of destructive power and assertion. In the Jātakas, the primary trace of this manner of creativity goes hand in hand with the authority of *bodhisattva*. This is only to say that an individual with the power of a saint could remarkably work out a structure of truth for himself and the other side of this situation would uniformly lie in the fact that concrete expression of an experience is generally beyond the determination of illusions, temptation and material perception, for that matter, the generation of a system of general truth, ideas, relation and primordial coherence becomes quite convincingly the matters of strength and activity. In *bodhisattva*, one can appropriately understand how a model in respect of each of these is obtained. Consider, for example, the following narrative from *Kimchanda Jātaka*:

> The Spirit recognized him and said, "You do not recognize me, but I was once your chaplain. This happiness that I enjoy in the night is due to you, as the result of my keeping half the first-day; while the suffering I experience by day is the result of the evil that I wrought. For I was set by you on the seat of judgement, and I took bribes and gave false decisions, and was a backbiter and in consequences of the evil that I wrought by day, I now undergo this suffering," and he uttered a couple of stanza.
>
> And so saying, he asked the ascetic why he had come here. The ascetic told all his story at length. "And now, holy sir," the Spirit said, "will you stay here or go away?" "I will not stay, I will return to my hermitage." The Spirit said, "Very well, holy sir, I will constantly supply you with a ripe mango," and by an exercise of his magic power he transported him to his hermitage, and, biding him dwell there contentedly, he exacted a promise from him and went his way. Thenceforth the Spirit constantly

> supplied him with the mango fruit. The ascetic, in the enjoyment of the fruit, performed the preparatory rites to induce mystic meditation and was destined to the Brahma-world.
>
> – Francis 1957: 109; *Kimchanda Jātaka*, p. 4

In this passage, the primary approach is how to cope up with internal and external forms of evil to conduct an action for the sake of better life. The action happens in the present moment of time, and, therefore, it quite carefully records the immediate perception. The king or *bodhisattva* is conceived through greater depth. He could understand what is wrong, and, therefore, he could also understand what the best is in a given situation. *Bodhisattva*, being a reincarnation of God, goes along and arrives at the tertiary form of truth. His success would depend on how his personal excellence gathers him into a mould of an extension of larger ideal situation. The other person who happens to be the minister of the king is also a suffering man since in his time he went for the misconducts. The second person withholds the expression of truth, and, in that way, he comes out with an exercise of the choices and preferences between the king and his courtier. The necessary connection of transmutation into purer and concrete being is established. While we look at this form of presentation, we could understand that in king and his courtier the extent of difficulty lies in communicating this urgency to the external world.

In that way we can understand that the *Jataka Tales* create an action through an opposition that is developed between good and evil and accordingly the point is established that only valid means of presenting a term for life is to make life virtuous, graceful, kind, generous and holy. The essential reality of whole action is goodness and *bodhisattva* is a perfect example of this goodness.

In *Jataka Tales*, the basic idea of presenting an opposition between good and evil is by creating definite structure of good and the evil. So far as good is concerned, the major forms which come to the notice of any reader are based on what the necessity that may be there to occasion the creation of good. In the Jātaka narratives, this idea is realized through the object and the subject hence it is also a direct object of perception and sensation. An individual, who stands upon the earth and seizes the various objects of earth, is thus directly recreated into them through their native consequence of effect. There is nothing that is left for any future observation and past association. What happens, happens with the opening of the eyes, and closing of the eyes in that way the effect of an object is to be recorded when observation is being exchanged through them to record an expression in the mind of an individual. The consolidation of sensory impression through the reversal of location and redirection is an important feature that deals with a definition of perception established in the observation. It is also denied that the creation of meaning through a commuted or committed correlation of the category is also quite not possible hence the life and the world must be levelled through the concentration of an action that is mounted. For this reason, the action that begins with the beginning of strong visual effect is to be considered as the necessary part of presentation of a term for meaning. For example, look at the following episode from *Kumbha Jātaka*:

> "The king, after putting the men to death, gave orders that the jars should be broken. But the cats, when the effect of the liquor wore off, got up and walked about and played." When they saw this, they told the king. The king said, "If it were poison, they would have died; it must be mead; we will drink it." So he had the city decorated, and set up a pavilion in the palace yard and taking his seat in this splendid pavilion on a royal throne with a white umbrella raised over it, and surrounded by his courtiers, he began to drink. Then Sakka, the king of heaven, said, "Who are there that in the duty of service to mother and the like diligently fulfil the three kinds of right conduct?" And, looking upon the world, he saw the king seated to drink strong drink and he thought, "If he shall drink strong drink, all India will perish: I will see that he shall not drink it." So, placing a jar full of the liquor in the palm of his hand, he went, disguised as a brahmin, and stood in the air, in the presence of the king, and cried, "Buy this jar, buy this jar." King Sabbamitta, on seeing him standing in the air and speaking after this manner, said.
>
> On hearing this the king, recognizing the misery caused by drink,

> was so pleased with Sakka that he sang his praises in two stanzas.
>
> Thus did Sakka admonish him and then returned to his abode in Heaven. And the king, abstaining from strong drink, ordered the drinking vessels to be broken. And undertaking to keep the precepts and dispensing alms, he became destined to Heaven. But the drinking of strong drink gradually developed in India.
>
> – Francis 1957: 96-97; *Kumbha Jātaka*, p. 7

In this situation the presentation of an action is done through constructing a relative simplicity in attitude and assertion, and, for that matter, the object and the subject are made to correspond each other. The object in the case is the imposition of a sanction on procreating an evil through wrong terms and absolutely wrong measures and the subject and the king and *bodhisattva* standing firmly in opposition to the situation. The necessity of developing a charter of demands through which the strength of wine is adjudged is excellent. The king first becomes a seeker and having become so, he goes on to taste the wine for the first time and gets intoxicated and falls asleep. This shows that the perception of the king is very much organized and concentrated inasmuch as he goes on to understand the nature of the evil embodied in the wine. The proposition is thus established that to become evil or to understand an evil one has to become like an evil and here we could see that there is complete transformation of an individual into an action. On the other hand, the strength of change is become a matter of exercising a choice or an option. The choice is reflected in how the method is reconstructed for a better knowledge and that perception could lead to a better sensation provided. There is an urgency and necessity to present the whole situation through meaningful terms. The developing action is not limited to this; rather it is expanded through the incoming of *bodhisattva* to pass a final judgement on this. It means that when there is truth and purity, the qualitative condition of perception and observation is so finally enriched that the individual is consciously developed. The appearance of *bodhisattva* is just to compensate this form. There is hardly any merit in proving the point that truth and honour are the necessary parts of the structure. The condition for emergence of truth is hidden in the practice of inventing a fact for reason and assertion. Reason is an act of upholding the validity of truth through exposition of fact in timeless situations, for that matter, it is the individual who locates this fact through a rediscovery of his fine instincts. We can understand that *bodhisattva* appears exactly at the framework of consciously apprehended time and motion hence he becomes normally elevated from the general objects, ordinary thoughts and material pursuits. Here goodness is an impression on concentrating the end of present time and beginning, and the infinity. To approach this matter in a more systematic manner, we will have to build up a structure through the evolution of time and the growth of divinity from absolute to new-absolute. The king who falls upon the intoxicating effect of wine is a material part of time arrangement and *bodhisattva* who appears on the scene is a permanent feature of the expansion of time. There is no opposition as such between the king and *bodhisattva*. *Bodhisattva* embraces and incorporates the king into his own form and enables him. This fact is very important with regard to an understanding of the Jātakas and other Indian narratives. Form and truth contained could be substantiated by saying that Indian narratives do not develop a concomitance of binary opposition rather the object and the subject are constantly in a state of transmutation.

> The king heard that the prince had returned and set out to meet him, and the prince, escorted by a great multitude, came and saluted the king. And he asked him, saying, "Dear son, how have you escaped from so terrible an ogre?" And he said, "Dear father, he is no ogre; he is your elder brother and my uncle". And he told him all about it and said, "You must go and see my uncle". The king at once ordered a drum to be beaten, and set out with a great retinue to visit the ascetics. The chief ascetic told them the whole story in full; how the child had been carried off by an ogress, and how instead of eating him she had brought him up as an ogre, and how they were related one to another. The king said, "Come, brother, do you reign as king". "No, thank you, Sire," he replied. "Then come and take up your abode in our park and I will supply you with the four requisites." He refused to come. Then the king made a settlement on a certain mountain, not far from their hermitage, and, forming a lake,

> prepared cultivated fields and, bringing a thousand families with much treasure, he founded a big village and instituted a system of almsgiving for the ascetics. This village grew into the town Cullakammasadamma.
>
> – Francis 1957: 268-69; *Jayaddisa Jātaka*, p. 19

In this episode, the suitability and position of the object and the subject are in harmony with the achievement of participation and involvement in the whole questioning, approval and disapproval. On the either side of the situation, we can think of *bodhisattva* constituting and creating enlargement of an ideal virtue and ideal action hence goodness is the solid effect. The way in which evil is constructed through radical sensuous perception is also quite remarkable. The apprehension of wine as symbol of evil suggests a perception that is mounted on the liquid that is contained yet is prone to dispersion. For this reason the viscosity of the liquid cannot be the necessary part of strength contained in the wine. Wine is important only because it intends a notion about flowing ceaselessly till it contains the object that has attracted its attention and in that way symbolical wine is the measurement of the worst that is to follow. The king, on one hand, and *bodhisattva*, on the other, explain the reason for their choices. The king, being a part of this world, does not succeed in rationalizing the consequence of perception arising out of a mandatory observation that he makes for the sake of wine. *Bodhisattva* comprehends the wine not as a finality but only as a beginning of the final cause. This approach serves the movement of action so much so that the decay of king on account of an evil is revived in the formation of an excellence in the logical virtue of *bodhisattva*. In the Jātaka stories, this issue has almost entirely been left for an uncertain notice. The merit of this observation lies in the fact that the constant mutation of object into subject or goodness into virtue supports the formation of a point of view that good thought and good thinking are ultimately born into the rational faculty of a man. It is all just a matter of coordinating the nobility of thought and thinking for the sake of some better equivalent. *Bodhisattva* is a high formation hence he could deprive himself of impermanence that emerges from deviant appearance. The logical question involved in the episode makes us realize that there is no point in comprehending the infinity of infinity and regression of regression rather from infinity one should return to reaffirmation of virtue as a principle. The necessity of creating a condition of virtue would be definitely based on virtue to inter-related situation first to propose a valid test for evil and second canonize the goodness as a principle of eternity and infinity. Here *bodhisattva* is both a geographical dimension and speculative formation who is equally placed in the conduct of the both.

In the Jātakas, the different conditions occurring in life are seen as interchangeable and interacted and for that matter evil cannot remain evil for so long. It has to turn into goodness and goodness, on the other hand, for a very long, has to remain goodness. It decays in it as an authority and as a commitment, and the time frame associated with each of these is different. Evil is shortlived, and, therefore, temporary while goodness is durable, therefore, tends to be permanent. *Bodhisattva* joins this as a form of thought and thinking and the laws he lays down are quite in harmony with this principle of life.

> Now in offering them to the queen, he said, "Lady, the elephant against whom you conceived a grudge in your heart for a trifling offence, has been slain by me". "Do you tell me that he is dead?" she cried. And he gave her the tusks, saying, "Be assured that he is dead: here are his tusks". She received the tusks adorned with six different coloured rays on her jewelled fan, and, placing them on her lap, gazed at the tusks of one who in a former existence had been her dear lord and the thought, "This fellow has come with the tusks he cut from the auspicious elephant that he slew with a poisoned shaft". And at the remembrance of the great Being she was filled with so great sorrow that she could not endure it, but her heart then and there was broken and that very day she died. – Francis 1957: 96; *Chaddanta Jātaka*, p. 30

The way in which the baser side of instinct is called upon to demotivate the purpose of commitment is noteworthy. The grudge of a lady is presented through the choices which have acted upon the experience and the choices are not only defunct but also discredited. We can perceive an action to be primarily mounted on the grudge and envious disposition of an individual whose purpose is to affect the sensibility so that the worth of virtue and evil could be understood and comprehended. The necessity of such a presumption lies plainly in the exceptional craving of the individual (man and woman) and the fact is constantly brought to notice of the individual that illusion can be worked out very well through prohibitory measures in which an individual is restrained not to express the contents of his actual experience rather to always express the unintended part of undesirable sensation. So far as the structure of the Jātakas is concerned, we can think of three major situations: intention, commitment and expression through resolution in the whole. A scheme is quite comfortably built around the authority of an individual who is a reborn God. *Bodhisattva*, being a reborn God, constructs a structure for intention, commitment and resolution by finding suitable individual, who could fall upon good and bad situations of this world. In the foregoing, we have clearly stated each of these at length and we have also concluded that individuals and *bodhisattva* form a different graduation for the authenticity of material illusion and transcendental reality respectively.

## III

In *The Pilgrim's Progress*, the narrative structure is smooth, harmonious and built around an opposition between goodness and evil. This binary opposition has been suggested through

A. Illusion

B. Appearance

C. Commitment

D. Resolution

In *The Pilgrim's Progress*, the condition of narrative is based on an application of personified situation in which each of the human categories is given an application in relation to each of the above. The central character of this narrative, Christian, who is a seeker of the truth, is constantly confronted with the illusion drawn from the material world inhabited by such deviant circumstances, doubt and obstinate. Christian pursues truth, honesty, generosity, freedom, emancipation and finally God. He is brought to life of action by such categorical forms as charity, prudence and piety. It is quite interesting to note that opposition between good and evil is securely the situation that creates fundamental motive of perception with regard to the structure of the narrative. Christian, being the central person, goes on and keeps suggesting that life that we live is not the life that we are required to live rather we should have been living a life that is only to be found in the soul of oneself since soul is the essential and principal goodness of the experience. The journey that Christian undertakes to perform is in fact his fight against the many illusions, which keep occurring in the form of wrath, greed, lust, desire and envy in this world. Beginning of such a journey is exclusively founded on an emergence from the material illusion in such a way that Christian vows not to enact the necessity of becoming a part of this life that is lived only at the expense of destruction and deprivation. The contents of action at the beginning favour a description through the concepts of illusion and appearance themselves. Illusion is an erotic presentation of an otherwise factual term whose perception and comprehension both are vague and arbitrary. In this case, the individual's move in the direction of a goal is by no means clear. In fact, there is an offer to benefit one by supporting the claim that the individual concerned is in a position to receive a due recognition from the external circumstances. The worth of reality is destroyed to such an extent that the facts are evolved into an altogether different direction. Christian could understand that beginning in such a difficult world is not only impossible but dangerous and risky also inasmuch as he would be simply called upon to always rediscover and reinvent himself. Association with an evil would definitely mean disappearance from the position of fact to whatever is meant to be the known, not fact. Christian exclaims with conviction:

> Christian: "I seek an 'inheritance, incorruptible, undefiled, and that fadeth not away,' and it is laid up in Heaven, and fast there, to be bestowed at the time appointed on them that diligently seek it. Read it so, if you will, in my book." –Bunyan 1960: 20

In this, we can understand that Christian is reviving the nativity of his conviction, and, therefore, he discards both the illusion and appearance in a temporal scheme. Time, for him, is a matter of endless inquiry and infinite search for truth in such a way that his actions go on to purify him. This act of purification is, in fact, an initiation that draws upon a presentation of a frame of work and action and in this situation work/action is in the manner of threat or imposition. In Christian's case, the objects of meditation (material illusion and the cause of meditation) both impose a necessity to generalize him in the context of this worldly wisdom. Fact is not meant to be darkness rather it is the light of the day that illumines the whole and brings the best for him. As an individual the conscience of Christian is really praiseworthy because his action rarely falls upon the urgency of association with the laser forms. Hence he expects at every point of time and illusion from within so as to put up a brave face before this world of illusion and imperfections. Christian could extend the length of his inquisition by making other allegorical forms like envy, obstinacy, evil to work in accordance with the idea of division and separation between good and evil. Hence he could mean to establish an ideal balance between those who create hurdles in the path of goodness and those who progress towards evil and meanness.

In the early part of the narrative, the scale of action and type of characterization approached by Bunyan make it very clear that an individual in the midst of uncertainly in life could have a fairer say in the reception of the goodness. An ideal individual is also in a position to proclaim the truth by vowing that his supreme goodness would be to reach God under any condition and in any circumstance. The beginning of an action on a note of proclamation clearly sums up the cyclical form of action in which the action announces admission, proclamation or address and continues through the obstruction yet once again comes back to the truth. This could be identified with the movement of earth around the sun in which there is a beginning at the point of origin and an end once again at the point of origin. In fact, Christian's announcement solely excludes him from the general crudeness of the nature and exposes him to the universal scheme of presentation in which the soul is capable of meeting God. This particular proclamation is the height of narrative technique adopted by the novelist. In this situation the character (Christian) is constantly made to submit him to the test of disadvantages, demerits, disassociation and fragmentation as determined by the mortal conditions in the life. Each of these disadvantages is very temporary yet comes squarely with power and force and disjoints anybody who could stand to it. Christian's position in this regard is revival and recovery inasmuch as he could perceive the sequence of disadvantages and could clearly and exactly decipher them. For example, look at the following:

> Christian: Then said Christian, "You make me afraid, but whither shall I fly to be safe? If I go back to mine own country, that is prepared for fire and brimstone; and I shall certainly perish there."
> – Bunyan 1960: 46

There can be two distinct positions that can be apprehended in the motive of Christian in dissolving resolution and committing himself to the strength of a superior passion. It follows from this that he constantly upgrades the resolution by upgrading the improved situation hence the intended action does not divert, rather it goes on to stretch itself with an unfolded motion and also by extending diverse regeneration of a sequence of perception. Home in this regard could be considered to be as a primary dysfunction associated with fall and disgrace while the journey is a motion in which the nature and the space both are acting in the manner of vertical forces to restore the different units in a new style and new manner. Christian's conception is in a process of multiplying himself at the sight of the intended division. The arithmetical form fits in the milieu of Christian so well that he synthesizes everything ranging from division to multiplication, and addition to subtraction. It is quite interesting to note that Christian could finally transmute everything into himself. The progress of Christian by the virtue of an action that clearly separates and demarcates him from the material conditions of the life is altogether noteworthy. In fact, it is better to say that Christian creates an absolute in himself so much so that he presents a scheme of totality in himself and this totality is best reflected in the way in which he absorbs the imperfect forms of life and turns them into finer stretch. In *The Pilgrim's Progress*, the arrangements of evil is constantly and exactly cyclical in such a way that the origin in end and end in origin are simultaneously achieved and simultaneously proposed through various coordinates along this circle. For example, look at the following:

> Then I saw in my Dream, that the Interpreter took Christian by the hand, and led him into a place, where was fire burning against a wall, and one standing by it always, casting much water upon it to quench it. Yet did the fire burn higher and hotter.
>
> Then said Christian, "What means this?"
>
> The Interpreter answered, "This fire is the work of grace that is wrought in the heart; he that casts water upon it, to extinguish and put it out is the Devil; but in that thou seest the fire, notwithstanding, burn higher and hotter, thou shalt also see the reason of that." So he had him about to the back side of the wall, where he saw a man with a vessel of oil in his hand of which he did also continually cast, but secretly, into the fire. Then said Christian, "What means this?" The Interpreter answered, "This is Christ, who continually with the oil of his grace, maintains the work already begun in heart; by the means of which, notwithstanding what the Devil can do, the souls of his people prove gracious still. And in that thou sawest, that the man stood behind the wall to maintain the fire; this is to teach thee that it is hard for the tempted to see how this work of grace is maintained in the soul. – Francis 1957: 269; Bunyan 1960: 37

The action that is intended is proposed through an antithetical form in that the ideas of being good and being bad are simultaneously approached and approved. The water and the fire being two allegorical forms connect the validity of proposal through intensity of participation equally obtained in each. Water is water because it spills the moment it is thrown hence under normal circumstances water cannot be the part of any concentrated endeavour. While fire contains an extent of concentration with a precise and defined geometrical length and pattern, the effect of concentration is massive, immense and unquestionably profound. This relativity of being viscous and being concentrated is something that distinguishes goodness of purpose and worthiness of pursuit. God is on the side of the fire and the water that is likely to be thrown on fire is to be called the devil and in that way the magnitude of remark is immensely comprehensible in that good and bad shall forever be standing in opposition to each other. The diversity of the situation is exceptionally rich because badness of badness and goodness of goodness can never be merited through similar paradigms. The author seems to be synthesizing the operation of content-oriented medium in the background of decontextualized situation where power and strength are surprisingly dissolved in a preparation to be effective and rich. It occupies a place in the scheme of attention of an observer who sees and puts forth a condition of judgement on the whole situation. The idea of exposing the virtue to content-oriented meaning and context-less medium is to say, in other words, that the depth of participation in an event by the creation of infinity on both of the sides would be a real account of presumption. While considering this fact one has to think of necessary connection between the speed of resolution and annihilation of an evil for the sake of a concentrated motion thereby producing strong effect in such a way that the movement of an object displaces both the individual and his equivalent action. Projection of water and fire has been the most important part of an antithesis absolutely confirmed through diversion of meaning on an infinite opposition. In *The Pilgrim's Progress* the idea of goodness and purity and even truth is quite interesting to know and understand. Goodness is an increase in the strength of perception while badness is a decrease or loss in the knowledge and hence the event that creates badness is likewise turned and moved along the closing coordinates. For this reason, the action of badness is generally marginal and closes after some time. Bunyan's wisdom in presenting the two sides of the situation is thoroughly explained when Christian comes across various people occupying various positions in this world. And the worth of position is such that each person is quite capable of motivating reason, and, even if, the reason is intended for the sake of something really very unethical and unreasonable, the question arises as to how an individual who is stylistically composed to ascertain if the pursuit is worth in an apparently unworthy and unholy circumstances. In other words, it would mean that conversion and diversion are likely to be brought to a union through a condition of endurance and patience. Situations such as this could only be a factor in the determination of a point of synthesis while the whole external circumstance is imbalanced, undetermined, uneven and odd. Success of such a scheme will have to be operated through a method of separation and distance. Union is synthesis between both the medium and the content and there is no doubt in suggesting that the merits of Bunyan's artistry complete the requirements of the terms.

## IV

In *Jataka Tales* and *The Pilgrim's Progress* the necessity of having a structure is felt in comprehensive and extreme concentration of individuals' events and the situations which generally compose a form and manner of exchange, interchange and change amongst every conceivable formation. In fact, it is better to say that the ideational, relational and fractional forms of the contents operate for the sake of a better function of the whole situation. In each of these narratives the entire structural form could be divided into the strength of the functioning of the following categories (Chart 1).

The appearance is a composition of the concentrated version of irrationality in which the medium and the context both exclude themselves in the presentation of the form. In that way, the context is not committed to propose any end in view rather it is worthy of being brought to unsystematic significance. In appearance, the method is absolutely precise in diverging the object as object, the subject as subject, and both the object and the subject themselves. An individual, who purports to classify a phenomenon by tending to make the meaning through the event, is not very successful, rather there is a fragmentation of purpose, intention, motive and conviction. The quality of appearance is generally inherent in the magnitude of strength created by the object and the subject through a series of imperceptions, occasioned through a dislocated experience right at the sight of disharmony of its presentation. In *Jataka Tales*, the

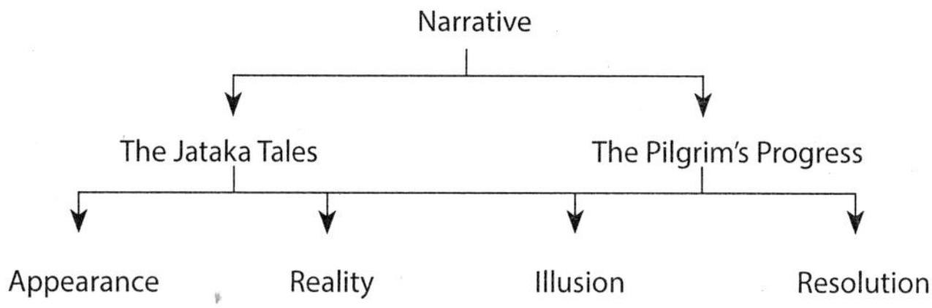


**Chart 1**

conception of appearance has a fair/logical precision because there is a generosity in granting permanence to those forms of presentation of an individual or an idea, or, even otherwise, an attitude that retains the functional authority just for a time being. *Bodhisattva* himself in the manner of a divine situation embodies to enlarge the material construction so as to wipe out the evil from the face of the earth. The narrative begins with a special reference to the generic category to which it belongs. The narrative of one generic system is also like the consolidated effect of subject and object creation so as to bring them before the eyes of the persons of the world. It is to be understood that *bodhisattva*'s synthesis is finally divided into what he could retain in the formal logic of object and subject both simultaneously. Narrative situation that exists in the Jātakas could well have a meaning and a purpose in the following graphical scheme (Chart 2).

The methods of appearance are inherent in the exposure of an object to the immensity of external situations, and, in this regard, it is worth the while to understand that an object is dissolved and recreated through consequence of perception and acquisition of the motive. Perception brings about sanctity in realizing the truth through the effect of various categories. For example, let us look at the following event in the Jātakas, contained in an episode from *Uraga Jātaka*:

> "Who, I wonder, is anxious to bring me down from my throne?" And on reflection he discovered that the heat was due to the force of virtue existing in these people, and being highly pleased he said, "I must go to them and utter a loud cry of exultation like the roaring of a lion, and immediately afterwards fill their dwelling place with the seven treasures". And going there in haste he stood by the side of the funeral pyre and said, "What

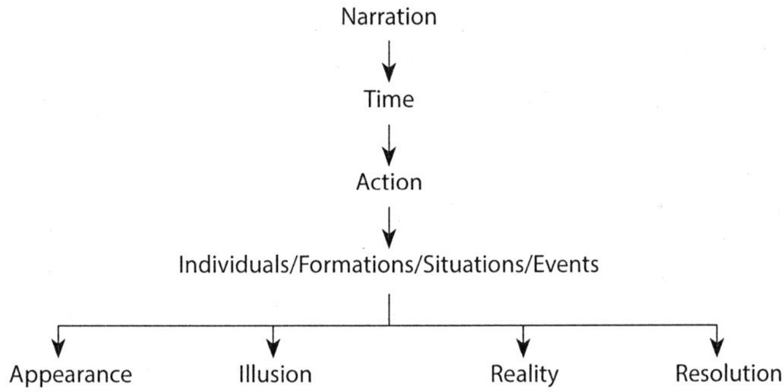


**Chart 2**

> are you doing?"
>
> "We are burning the body of a man, my lord."
>
> "It is no man that you are burning." he said. "Methinks you are roasting the flesh of some beast that you have slain."
>
> "Not so, my lord." they said. "It is merely the body of a man that we are burning."
>
> Then he said, "It must have been some enemy."
>
> The *bodhisatta* said, "It is our own true son, and no enemy".
>
> "Then he could not have been dear as a son to you."
>
> "He was very dear, my lord."
>
> "Then why do you not weep?"
>
> – *Uraga Jātaka*, p. 109

The manner of presentation creates a well developed system of recognition and by establishing the fact that presentation to the material system is the best way to anticipate a decay and disintegration of this material world. In the present context, we are made to understand that there is a subject that is appearing before us and is cast in a mould of recognition and acceptance and that is why the worth what it carries is concretely embodied in the reflection of truth in his utterance. Truth, in the context, could be understood to be a part of sequence of function to obtain a nativity in utterance. *Bodhisattva* begins the effect of judgement through the explication of a consequence in each of the stresses that he creates. To understand *bodhisattva* in this situation is to see how the language as one of the categories is brought nearer through revival and acceptance on the part of the each of the person's intention. There is nothing marginal or peripheral about the time frame and time sequence that he develops. One has to understand that presentation of an object by *bodhisattva* is primarily by receiving the object as a temporal situation hence there is a great success on his part to canonize him as a model amongst those who lose their conscience in the ignorance created by the illusory form and illusory perception. There is a commitment in dissolving an object as a divine part of included form hence object reappears with renewed strength in both the assimilation and deviance. In this narrative episode, the kith and kin of the dead person are not weeping – kith/kin hence the object and the subject both are composing a will. The largeness of the situation purports to create validity in saying that the effect of attitude to rationalize the will is approximately equal to the utterance or complimentary evidence suggested by the material beings. The progress of action in the event of appearance is proportionately dispersed over the ethical forms generated, created and sustained by the participants in this episode. For example, look at this conversation:

> "We are burning the body of a man, my lord."
>
> "He was very dear, my lord."
>
> "Then why do you not weep?
>
> – *Uraga Jātaka*, p. 109

In this we can understand attitude for the sake of resolution adopted through a purpose that is hidden in the strength of the whole, and, therefore, the primary effect of assertion is compounded through direct change into the nearness of the content. On the other hand, the time frame of the situation is invented in the reciprocal balance that affects communication across vertical and horizontal identities created in such things as fairness, exchange, interchange and recreation. Object is precisely equidistant from the rotations marked by the subject, and, therefore, the first assertion is right at the identification of first person himself in saying that we are burning the body of a man. The speaker would like to convey the idea that there is a perception that is really appearing through the measure of an event into resolvable parts, and, therefore, the intention of the speaker is to carry on the largest part of the action together authenticated in the subject and the predicate. The beginning that is made through full-scale and wholesome action by indicating the size of an action contained in both the subject and the predicate is a remarkable feature of the narration created in the Jātakas. Sometimes, we wonder as to how a fragment of conviction opens up a prospect of dissolution of an experience into attitude and leaves the effect of time itself? The answer to this question may perhaps lie in our understanding of values encoded in the absolute parts of the assertion, for example, look at the following: "He was very dear, my lord./Then why do you not weep?" (*Uraga Jātaka*, p. 109). In this opening of an inquisition and the end of sequence that creates inquisition is remarkably the same hence the lengthening of the time spent in occupying an elevated function is quite surprisingly concrete and very formal in the situation.

To understand the effect of appearance as a normal yet considerable style of recognition of a presentation, one has to merit the situation by saying that in the narratives like Jātakas, the events are chronologically so perfect and stable that their progress and culmination into succeeding event is precisely a case of reception with greatest possible strength. In the Jātakas nearly all the individuals are created out of the material effect generated by the appearance of the divinity on the earth in the form of *bodhisattva* at the centre. He (*bodhisattva*) creates the perception while outside the contents of perception gather themselves up and enact an attitude, motive, reason and image hence the embodiment created in such a way behaves and acts with a maximum attention on identifying and proposing a structure for perception. The manner of perceiving a situation in the Jātakas amounts to composing a variety of equivalents as models for the glance of the eyes on the external subjects. When *bodhisattva* goes on to set his foot on the earth in a queer fashion, the observations are not essentially proposed and conducted through the internalization of the facts, *bodhisattva* could only perceive the rigid sequence of personal and impersonal categories and thus exactly turn them to be the better forms above knowledge of the whole situation. The form of divinity in *bodhisattva* is realistically open to the presentation of a definite meaning of actions and for the purpose, conceives an equal wisdom in each and every formation. The method of perception by God or by reincarnated God would be quite clearly on a grand scale of rationalization, and, therefore, what appears before the eyes, what goes on before the eyes, what was there before the eyes, and what shall be there before the eyes will have the function in the same centre of the mind. We can just take the situation to be very effective through the denotation of God as God and God as a human being. While God is a god, the phenomenon of rationalization of the experience is absolutely a motive of an absolute, therefore, the question, "why do you not weep?", could suggest the enlargement of perception by the worth of denotation itself. In so far as denotation is the real worth of reality and exactly explores an interrelationship between a noble individual and extended space. This relationship is very systematically created and attained in the Jātakas:

> The Bodhisatta proclaimed by beat of drum, "No living creature is to be put to death". The Yakkhas were enraged against the Bodhisatta at losing their offerings, and calling together an assembly of their kind in the Himalayas, they sent forth a certain savage Yakkha to slay the Bodhisatta. . . . The Bodhisatta on seeing the Yakkha thought, "Why in the world is he standing here? Is it to protect me, or from a desire to slay me?" . . . On hearing the words of Bodhisatta the Yakkha said, "Great king, I am not stationed here to guard you; I came minded to smite you with this blazing mass of iron, but through fear of Sakka I dare not strike you." *Ayakuta Jātaka*, p. 96

The arrangement of action in terms of appearance is clearly exclaimed through visual and non-visual motivations and even auditory and non-auditory significance is enlisted in the visual part. The sight is brought to an actual confirmation of the identity of meaning hence the manner of exposing the experience to the reality is very direct and perceptible. *Bodhisattva*, on account of being God and *yakṣa* in the capacity of a demon could resolve and synthesize the formal strength of presentation. *Yakṣa* appears before *bodhisattva* and in that way delivers an attitude of significance to the permanently logical effects of meaning emerging from *bodhisattva*. The scale of perception primarily accepts the motive in orienting the cause of perception through a process of converting attitude and ideology both on the part of the subject and the object. And for this reason, the necessity of inquiring a virtuous model, the divinity, does not have to work out a scheme as it normally happens rather it introduces itself in the generous framework of an otherwise unruly and chaotic situation in the above. *Bodhisattva* by breaking the barriers of the time that places himself before the ineffective condition in which the imposition of appearance is proposed to be defined through underlying sets of compulsions. For example, the Buddha says "Yakkha why in the world is he standing here, Is it to protect me or from a desire to slay me".

The question now arises as to how *bodhisattva* marks a conduct for his appearance in a compulsive situation such as this where force of submission and the strength of opposition both equal one another. *Bodhisattva*'s comprehension of the time is as an eternal principle always going, always passing and always returning for a credit to insert and fix up substantially a permanent conduct in the sanctity of the ethos. And by that standard, we can have no difficulty in composing a functional ethic for *bodhisattva* himself and the other point that we can think of noting is how the appearance resolves itself through the facility of conjunction acting as a motive of association between the object and the subject. Look at the following example:

> Yakkha said, "Great king, I am not stationed here to guard you; I came minded to smite you with this blazing mass of iron, but through fear of Sakka I dare not strike you."
>
> – *Ayakuta Jātaka*, p. 97

The principle of association expounded here by *bodhisattva* could be held to be the basic cause in exposing and evaluating the experience. The idea of conjunction is a slow but definite measurement of reality in one of the primary assertions of the fact. Style and manner of concentrating the effect of appearance by locating a series of comprehensive varieties of assertions in a very discreet form the subject and the object both are comprehensible in such a way that object's meaning, subject's meaning with regards to the attending action are concretely functionalized by approaching values for both of the generic forms, for example, consider the following from *Gaṅgamāla Jātaka*:

> The king said to his minister, "Go have my friend shaved and bathed and adorned, and bring him back", then did so. The king divided his kingdom in two and gave him half: but they say that he took the northern half from love of his half-penny. He was called King Half-penny. They ruled the kingdom in friendship and harmony. One day they went to the park together. After amusing themselves, King Udaya lay down with his head in king's Half-penny's lap. He fell asleep, while the attendants were going here and there enjoying their amusements. King Half-penny thought "why should I always have only half the kingdom? I will kill him and be sole king".
>
> Feeling that this thought, rising again and again, would lead him on to the evil deed, he threw the sword on the ground and woke the king. "Pardon me, O king", he said and fell at his feet. "Friend, you have done me no wrong." "I have, O great king: I did such and such a thing." "Then, friend, I pardon you: if you desire it, be sole king, and I will serve under you as viceroy." He answered, "O king, I have no need of the kingdom, such a desire will cause me to be reborn in evil states: the kingdom is yours, take it: I will become an ascetic: I have seen the root of desire, it grows from a man's wish." –p. 268

We can understand that *bodhisattva* is launching himself on a rather rational pragmatic ethos of the conduct, and, therefore, opts for an association that is completely mutual and interchangeable. The effect of correspondence between *bodhisattva* and the newly-found friend is to establish a commitment for speeches and utterances, and, consequently, the perception generated retains the combined appearance of both the motive and reason. The enlargement of effect is built around by strengthening the model codes like shaved, bathed, adorned, friendship, harmony, so as to create the codes of incentives. On the other hand, there are codes of disincentives like jealousy, greed and enmity. For example, look at this:

> The king said to his ministers, "Go, have my friend shaved and bathed and adorned, and bring him back". They did so. The king divided his kingdom in two and gave him half.
>
> King Half-penny thought, "Why should I always have only half the kingdom? I will kill him and be the sole king."
>
> – *Gaṅgamāla Jātaka*, p. 268

Both motive and reason obtained as a sequence of logic are bound together by the conjunction of inception and deception. In the explanation given by *bodhisattva* for being so cordial and sympathetic to the whole is to attribute comprehensive values in a friend who has not overcome his primary temptations. This is to say that the effect of coordination amongst two different values is to suggest that *bodhisattva* is an exceptionally immutable form of appearance in both the object and the subject while the position occupied by him in extensive faculty externally related to the space is completely identified as the prolongation of smooth and regular contents. The idea of influence suggested in this is important for two reasons. In the first place, the relative composition of the realistic and realizable features occurs approximately at a distance where situation is assisted through marginal variation in subject–object relationship. Therefore, when *bodhisattva* asks his friend to accept the gift of half of the kingdom, we can only record the merit of his own appearance. The concept of appearance in that way is reversible to upgrade and enlarge the identity by sanctifying the whole necessity of concretely embodying the meaningful form to the largest possible audience.

## V

In *The Pilgrim's Progress*, the idea of appearance is also linked to the growth of an individual but in such a way that the material form and the ennobled form are regularly and constantly interchangeable hence the idea of unique truthful form hardly exists at the centre of formation. There lies a material individual, who lives and breathes in this world; and from that position he forms his own conception of the world and God. It is better to say that the event of appearance is remarkably concentrated and synthesized through a worldly individual whose primary form is figural. The necessity of characterization by this means builds up unique features. The employment of the suggestive terms to indicate a manner of projection at the tertiary level is one of the features that commands the interest in the development of action in this novel. To say more frankly, John Bunyan develops a notion of allegorical formation by purporting a sense of both presentation and appearance in the visible and invisible categories. It is thus the expression of one category and its subsequent resolution brings about a symmetry and growth in the narrative. The choice of allegory as a viable method of characterization is something that has to be approved and consolidated later as a matter of meaning creation. And by this standard, the characters, which appear in this narrative, Christian, Faith, Hope, Doubt, Evangelical and Obstinate, are also at the same time absolute forms of consciousness. There can be a method in comprehending the situation by this standard and we will say that the effect of reception of both the perception and consciousness by Christian and others exposes the reality of truth formation in Christian and truth displacement in Obstinate, Doubt and others. This sense of commitment and fidelity on the one hand, and deviance and exclusion on the other, is definitely a matter of imposition in which the Soul is hopefully the final determinant. The scale of appearance is necessarily in *The Pilgrim's Progress* a subject of multiple divisions because of the fact that Christian is an agent of crisis and this crisis begins right at the beginning of the Christian as a character. He feels the turmoil so as to guide himself properly. The two major forms of this appearance(s) have the following names – first material and the second immaterial. In the material part of the situation, Christian undergoes a reduction of his basic identity in that he could not find any strength whatsoever in his categorical precision and perfection so much so that he renders each into an indefinite formation. The worth of being material is also the worth of being opened to the external space by the virtue of constant displacement of individual in the form of an object in such a way that he cannot determine his position to come out with a solution to this. He goes on to exchange the terms of displacement throughout the time span he contemplates and commutes for himself. In *The Pilgrim's Progress*, this interaction and interplay strengthens the individuality of Christian. For example, look at the following:

> "I looked then and saw a man named Evangelist coming to him, and asked, "Wherefore dost thou cry?" He answered, "Sir, I perceive, by the book in my hand, that I am condemned to die and after that to come to judgement; and I find that I am not willing to do the first, nor able to do the second."
>
> Then said Evangelist, "Why not willing to die since this life is attended with so many evils?" The man answered, "Because I fear that this burden that is upon my back will sink me lower than the grave, and I shall fall into Tophet. And, sir, if I be not fit to go to prison, I am not fit (I am sure) to go to judgement and from thence to execution; and the thoughts of these things make me cry."
>
> Then said Evangelist, "If this be thy condition, why standest thou still?" He answered, "Because I know not whither to go." Then he gave him a parchment roll, and there was written within, "Fly from the wrath to come". – Bunyan 1960: 18

The form of narration mainly speaks of two ideational forms. One is Christian and the other is Evangelist. In Christian, the formation of idea as a principle of authority is remarkably complete, and, therefore, he does not mean to combine the function of an experience. And for that matter, the inquisition with regard to the worth of experience is immediately resolved as a preference for distinctive attitude. The first important distinction is the certainty of impressions recorded as formal event, and, therefore, there is a greater success in identifying the absolute credentials of position, preference and acquisition of merit-oriented value. Preference for an excellent personality involved in the preparation of both the realistic and prospective plans for life is the truth of value-oriented distinction. One can very well understand that this is the only actual composition of merit that traces the effect of resolution. And for this purpose, Christian concentrates on the advantageous and beneficial motives found all around him. The magnitude of concentration is effective only through an enlarged form that associates his conviction with the changing intensity of unrealistic external commitments. In this regard, it seems worth the while to examine how Christian explores the similarities of condition in both the variants and equivalents that he opts for his own surplus. The first important situation that appears before us is clearly expressed in the way in which the succession of variants appropriately adds to the maximum of value and leaves only a little to the discontinuous as being worthless and unmerited. The appearance is recorded structurally through following three methods:

I. Identification,
II. Evaluation, and
III. Expression.

The first approach that leads to identification is invariably the selection of right individuality. This is the most important occasion in which Christian graduates himself into a scale of association whose function is to grant an approval to him hence it becomes, in reality, an affirmation of himself by himself. To achieve a purpose for necessity in developing a form for this, Christian always goes hand in hand with cruder perception to bring about a change in his ideal perception. This may be quite systematically an effort to rearrange the lost contents and achieve the point of primacy in asserting himself. It can be said with accuracy that appearance of Christian is completely an ideal expression meant for the sake of a new identity and a new name. We can look at the composite relevance of the whole situation by marking out some primary features like for example Christian is successfully assertive in disposing the condition with an adequate knowledge of goodness and badness in them and the length of appearance is equal to the meaning of perception, for example, look at the following:

Christian: "Is this the way to the Celestial City?"

Shepherd: "You are just in your way."

> Christian: "How far is it thither?"
>
> Shepherd: "Too far for any, but those that shall get thither indeed."
>
> Christian: "Is the way safe or dangerous?"
>
> Shepherd: "Safe for those for whom it is to be safe, 'but transgressors shall fall therein.'"
>
> Christian: "Is there in this place any relief for pilgrims that are weary and faint in the way?"
>
> Shepherd: "The Lord of these mountains hath given us a charge, 'Not to be forgetful to entertain strangers.' Therefore the good of the place is before you."
>
> – Bunyan 1960: 110

The subject of introspection and inquisition is built around an inception of inquisition and subsequently its reception through a consequential expression. Christian sees the glimpse of the new world, and on seeing this he immediately modifies his experience so as to bring him to larger and the largest equivalent. It is necessary to see how interior form of individuality is subjected to a correlation through the typical sign system marked in the authenticity of the questions. The questions are the elevation of potentials to resolve the condition of abstraction in both the object and the subject. With this motive in view, Christian multiplies active formation in his sensibility. The first formation is the authority of wonder, the second is the authority of curiosity and the third is the authority of doubt. In these three, Christian is equally dignified and elevated. He does not allow one inquisition to be suppressed by the other or relegated by the other, or, even otherwise, dissolved by the other. He simply enacts terms for continuity, progress and growth. A man as an individual and an individual as a man are distinct forms to associate separately as the external variation created in the manhood and individuality hence it cannot be as to how and why synchronic condition finally emerges as a measure of Hell to rescue Christian from the eminent fall. It is brought to the notice that purpose of appearance is inclined in the necessity to preserve the functioning of stretch of individuality right at the beginning and till the end. The exposition of Christian at the beginning is based on his success with regard to the convergence principle. And for this, he could bring about a continuity of enrichment of different shades of personality. And, for that matter, there is a commitment for the sake of expressing right content of the absolute at the right moment of time. The process of evaluation adopted and executed is precisely segmental and discursive. For this purpose, there is a segment created in the major category. For exact and appropriate refinement in the situation, Christian therefore, goes on to distribute his categorical intentions through an evidence of diversion in the major forms and major contents. At the beginning, he could see difficulty in the path that leads to the heaven yet he could also finally build up a defence through complete meaning expressed in a complete category. For this reason, there is no difference between acquisition of perception and expression of perception. This is a rather different mode of constructing a situation independently through a simultaneous emergence of the authority of personality. It is also sometimes related to an imposition through purely denotative formation of absolute meaning. For example, look at the following:

> Christian: "Not I," said Christian. "I have heard of this place before now, and how many have there been slain; and besides, that treasure is a snare to those that seek it, for it hindereth them in their pilgrimage." Then Christian called to Demas, saying, "Is not the place dangerous? Hath it not hindered many in their pilgrimage?"
>
> Demas: "Not very dangerous, except to those that are careless." But withal, he blushed as he spake.
>
> Christian: Then said Christian to Hopeful, "Let us not stir a step, but still keep on our way."
>
> Hopeful: "I will warrant you, when By-ends comes up, if he hath the same invitation as we, he will turn in thither to see."
>
> – Bunyan 1960: 100

In this situation there is a possibility that narrative events presuppose an order of authenticity in composing a sequence in commitment, conjunction and perception. Christian is close to perceive a necessity in upholding truth by a marginal abstraction of the perception. For this reason, he inquires into the very logic of thought and accordingly he proceeds to summarize the views contained in extreme situations. For example, in the above narrative, he shows his deeper understanding of the thought/action contained in the decision with regard to movement ahead and movement behind. The motion of authority is subjected to the motion of certainty precisely to temper the conviction with resultant meaning. There are two definite ways of these resultant situations. First is the inquisition that takes place in the manner of external impositions in which two sides chiefly present themselves. In the second place, Christian annihilates the procedural acceptance of very bad and very good by comprehending the superlative authority of the given situations, and, therefore, his involvement in the new situation becomes comparatively interactive in nature. Second, Christian could see that imposition of the right and left and even on the centre are not always made to carry the same value, for example, lure of temptation and intensity of truth both carry unequal assortment of value and there is always success on the part of Christian to recognize this problem.

## VI

The individual form in the Jātakas and *The Pilgrim's Progress* is determined through a very careful and conscious recognition of the native and natural strength of individual, therefore in each of the narrative discourses, the length of an individual, by the standard of expression, conduct and assertion, is precisely sometimes infinite and some time cyclical in nature. In the Jātakas, the individual, who happens to be the central character, is also a god, who has reborn to correct the deformities of life and by that standard he is the best among the best. This particular scene adopted in the Jātakas creates two important functions for the character. In the first place, the character is both ways round because he receives what he gets, he gets what he poses, and he poses what he creates, and in that way he assumes an existence in nearly all the four dimensions of temporal situation. This effect of presentation is derived from a well-known situation in which an individual is supposed to be in three implicit categories – "I", "Myself" and the

"Universe" which are recognized to be the three material/non-material phases of the existence. On the other hand, in *The Pilgrim's Progress* the presentation of an individual is sometimes suggestive and sometimes denotative. When it is denotative, it is also vertical; when it is suggestive, it is horizontal. We can understand that individuality of the Christian is precisely very denotative in nature because he does not present himself through experiential movement, and, therefore, he is not limited to presentation through various options. One of the issues involved in this scheme of expression is that Christian brings about an appearance before himself through both auditory and visual effects, and, of which, auditory significance has a larger concentration so far as distribution of an expression is concerned. Nevertheless hyper-imaginative effects created by Christian regulate the division of his enriched categories and save him from ruin and disintegration.

Individuality, so far as these two narrative situations are concerned, could be best understood in the context of visible order and organization that are many faceted and appear at each of the regular intervals of the time. The position of the time is slightly advanced so as to develop an organization in the framework of presentation. In fact, time regulates the content of motion hence it always makes the character purposely oriented for the sake of revival, induction, inception and incorporation into the act of involvement, comprehension and concentration. There can be two separate ways to state the function of time in authorizing an individual to make out an absolutely total conjunction. In the first place, individual is brought before the universe, the life and the world in such a way that immensity is exposed for the sake of a character to review him, and having revived to induct these principle and laws of synthesis which are constantly wavering and graduating along different coordinates in the universe. External space is only a limitation, therefore, it does not substantiate as to how content is received or terminated in accordance with decay and creation of formative perception and acquisitive cognition in the visible part of the space. Individual is expected to be always in a position to turn any perception, inference or judgement to his benefit on the whole. The situation is explained on the basis of certain cohesive contents through which preceding and succeeding parts of the universe standing just before and after the individual propose the maximum meaning for the person. In the Jātakas and *The Pilgrim's Progress*, this situation is really manifest with all accuracy while these two great works of art examine the nature of individual in different cultural environments of the East and the West. In *Jataka Tales*, an individual, who happens to be the character at the same time, is expected to be very flexible and in possession of a world view that should prompt him to look at the humanity as an infinite addition, regeneration and multiplication of the best part of experience, imagination, thought and the language. It could only be a matter of enriching absolutely the part of any category so that the best content is received in the form of a concrete universal with a focus concentrated and always functional. This is to say that the formation that appears on the earth as a god or a man should have the necessity to retain a sign for continuity in that he multiplies the addition of virtue and never substracts the proportions required for balance, and, in that way, the individual is qualified to become someone very significant and exclusive. In the Jātakas, the idea of connecting an individual with a focus on functional exposure to the world that really seems to be decadent and gloomy is conceived. *Bodhisattva* is one such character in whom we can understand the function of absolute which is modified just for the sake of awareness, recognition, identification and improvisation. And, it is hardly out of place to say that individual in *bodhisattva* is simultaneously a factual orientation for the sake of nearly complete transformation in all the four dimensions. For him the external world is a necessity of confirming the reality and the inner world is very exclusive to the propriety and meaning that this reality creates, hence *bodhisattva* is a man and a god. In so far as he is a man, he derives the strength from exposing the reality to the bare necessity of the life, and, for that matter, he could denote the facts rather than the figure and the object rather than the subject. This capacity of denotation of a fact and the object is one of the virtues that is associated with the form of God. On the other hand, *bodhisattva*'s existence as a god is a process of evolution and it is not quite surprising to see his position as a god is derived from the empirical necessity of worldly and material life. The combinations of these two oppositional necessities determining and governing the ideals for life are so beautifully brought together in the formation of *bodhisattva*. It is not ironical to point out how the urgency of the situation is committed for the sake of a projection that definitely defines a perspective for man that is God, not God who is a man. There cannot be any logic or variance between cohesion of these two structures. In fact, God in man and man in God are developed throughout *Jātakakathāvalī* as an absolute categorical structure, and, in this, one can understand the novelty of characterization to view the matter in another extensive scale. One will have to look at the particular conception of individual or individuals brought out in the Jātakas. In *Jātakakathāvalī*, the strength of determination of a living form is perceived as a case in structure for any individuals and, therefore, it is a constant enrichment of the category that may bring up an idea of man and the individual. Man is certainly a part of illusion, disorder, unreality and temptation regardless of position and direction occupied by him. It does not matter if the individual is facing the frontal or dorsal side of imminent temptation. He is bound to be caught in the unworthy settlement. It is because of this that man is unsafe and insecure. The question of man's position occupied right at the time of action either on the left or on the right becomes very important. The right side of illusion is a fall in such a way that the man is not in a position to revive himself. While the left side of illusion is a greater fall that practically annihilates the judgemental framework inside the primary faculties of the man. In this regard, we can state with conviction that in man both motive and reason are in a state of continuous disintegration and the only hopeful thing that happens is occasional revival through the restoration of facilities. In the Jatakas, *bodhisattva* carries both the comprehension and enlargement of motive and reason; therefore, he could confirm the best part of appearance and the greatest part of reality that could befit the welfare of an individual. The basic intention of *bodhisattva* is not to discredit the cause or the effect attending any serious manifestation or man stationed in this material world. His structure is so consolidated with regard to experience and perception that he replaces the weaker contents of the cause and deprivation that destroys the expression of effect. The goals of rationality established by *bodhisattva* are very primary, practical and full of practical wisdom; accordingly, the best way to make a bad a good is by persuasion, sympathy, consolation and solace. It could never be the other way round. Hence the theory of binary opposition is rejected altogether. Look at the following:

> "The earth is collapsing," they answered.
>
> "Who saw it collapsing?" he said.
>
> "The elephants know all about it," they replied.
>
> He asked the elephants. "We don't know", they said, "the lions know." But the lions said, "We don't know, the tigers know." The tigers said, "The rhinoceroses know." The rhinoceroses said, "The wild oxen know." The wild oxen, "The buffaloes." The buffaloes, "the elks." The elks, "the boars." The boars, "the deer." The deer said, "We don't know, the hares know." When the horses were questioned, they pointed to one particular hare and said, "This one told us".
>
> So the Bodhisatta asked, "Is it true, Sir, that the earth is breaking up?"
>
> "Yes, Sir, I saw it," said the hare.
>
> "Where," he asked, "were you living, when you saw it?"
>
> Then he told them the whole story, and said, "Don't be afraid." And having thus reassured the herd of beasts, he let them go. Verily, if it had not been for the Bodhisatta at that time, all the beasts would have rushed into the sea and perished. It was all owing to the Bodhisatta that they escaped death."
>
> – *Daddabha Jātaka*, p. 50

## VII

The status of narrative structure in respect of *Jataka Tales* and *The Pilgrim's Progress* could be assessed primarily through an equivalent idea of thematic technique, characteral formation and speech orientation developed within these two narrative situations. In each, the formation of total and absolute experience to project an individual perception is very remarkable and significant, and, for that matter, it is the individual himself who constitutes the code of motivation and experience. This is to say that the purpose of forming an experience for the sake of creation of an appropriate form/object/subject/individual is to regulate the scale and strength of transformation that come always in consequence of the change of an object into event. It is with this idea in mind that both *Jataka Tales* and *The Pilgrim's Progress* bring about a necessity of the fulfilment of persuasive ideal. In this, the projection of the situation is such that the issue of perception, is, also, at the same time, reciprocal in the manner of this reception and to return to the observer for the sake of communication between the two objects holding an equivalent status in two different circumstances. This approval of the situation is very realistic and factual. Similarly, in characterization and speech discourse, the strength of perception befits the entire range of expression. Communication in Jātakas and *The Pilgrim's Progress* is based on the concept of commitment, honour, trust, fidelity, truth and aptitude. *Bodhisattva*, for example, is one in whom the motives are primarily purified to the extent that the individual himself is capable of constructing an independent system of his own. This system becomes a concrete universal for him. The conditions of communication between the object and the medium with regard to an individual are carried on by a method of vertical/horizontal exchange in which the observer and the listener both have not more than two terms for motive as well as verbal expression. It is because of this the utterance increases the validity of making available the conceptual form at both the ends.

## VIII

Thematic concern is awareness with regard to the objects and situations, which go on to create a valid function for the action, are accidentally located in individual term and individual figures. In *Jataka Tales*, meaning of primary situation is exposed to every possible movement felt within the growth of perception mounted high on reception of a native situation. In the entire range of presentation, we could find one and only one individual to develop both inductive and deductive function by arranging and organizing a system of multiplication for himself, and, therefore, the same individual commits an association and conjunction from another minor forms and variations. To this extent, *bodhisattva* could seem to constitute a model in him for a meaning and definition of both man and God. The ideal form is rearranged for the sake of the crisis felt in giving a proper functioning of the live situations. In this way, order, truth, commitment, sincerity, devotion, dedication, involvement and the like become chief instruments and principal vehicles for systematically harmonizing an act of strength in the life. *Bodhisattva* assumes a position of distinction in such a way that he is in a capacity to both express and receive the content and the medium of the units that stretch them for order and synthesis in any primary disorder felt by simple person. While it is received in its primary contents by *bodhisattva*, there can be two ways to understand the situation. First, the primary significance that accrues and devolves on *bodhisattva* is in the ultimate nature of the event, and, second, the multiple forms that are created through *bodhisattva* generate immense possibility for the functioning of narrative situation. Every event has a meaning of its own and presentation of the life conditions is given extraordinary expression. We can look at the story of a priest, who took bribe and gave false judgement and the forester who discovered strong drink causing ruin and decay or royal elephant having two wives, or a king anxious for a goodness and truth or a husbandman looking for his straight option, a prince who is struck with leprosy or an unrighteous king reproved by a tree spirit or an archer displanning wonderful feats of skill in shooting or a certain king being reborn in the Nāga world. We have the opportunity to view the situation in such a way that communication is both real and factual, truthful and convincing, *bodhisattva* as a principal agent of transformation suggests the possibility of rearrangement of compulsive skill into an active skill. And this rearrangement is brought about by re-enacting himself through himself, and, therefore, it begins with the man so eager to know the cause of evil and divinity who is so keen to uproot the cause of evil, and, in that way, it is possible to understand the event of transformation taking place simultaneously for the sake of *bodhisattva* and also for the sake of suffering humanity infested with instinctual fallacies. Commitment of *bodhisattva* is unusual, and is in due proportion of the magnitude that he encompasses. He appears right at the moment the ruin is to commence, therefore, his role must be viewed as being a sympathizer and a regulator, and a synthesizer of each and everything.

Projection contained in the presentation of individuality has two concentrated forms. In the first place, the presentation of an evil or a badness or something that is decadent or defunct either in the life or in the manner or even in the scheme of things, is, by merit, a source of benefit both for a lay individual and for the supreme individual. To view the progression of the events in that way is to say that the origin of event is made right at the point at which the scope of addition, association or multiplication is really immense and noteworthy. It follows from this that the origin of action is circumstantially, situationally and conditionally inter-associative in nature, and opts for inter and intermediate associations throughout the path of progression. The basic contention involved in such a projection is simply to say that the point of origin recovers a model of communication between the medium and the context, and the medium and the content and for an effective progression, this situation is quite imminent. In *Jataka Tales*, the inquisitions are very affirmative in nature to the extent that each tale opens the possibility of assurance, solace and commitment, and in that way the four shades of expression are logically combined. *Bodhisattva* is an effective actor, who performs mutation and de-mutation, evolution and devolution of ascending compulsion or descending resolution and makes it acceptable to each and everybody. It appears as if the origin of *bodhisattva* is very much there in the denotative capacity of the objects which go on to observe and experience. We can understand from this that the beginning of a tale is marked by both exposition and resolution in such a way that the exposition contains a character who anticipates a decline or fall in terms of a motive and no sooner than this motive of decline, fall, deterioration sets in, we can have an appearance through presentation or individual form in *bodhisattva*. And the last part of the narrative is primarily extended to the association of *bodhisattva* in his standard form with the ordinary individual who is undergoing decline, disgrace and displacement of some sort through predestination or destination as a matter of necessity. This association of *bodhisattva* with an individual brings about transformation of the whole situation and brings forth what we can call the conclusion. Requirement for a theme is met with by expanding the law of association, addition and conjunction. It appears to be quite remarkable to have an origin in which value is encoded as a sign, hence when individual falls into disgrace, he does not approach *bodhisattva* rather through symbolical perception. *Bodhisattva* is automatically associated with the persons. Here, the form of *bodhisattva* acts as a sign and whatever comes in its way is added to by the intelligence and wisdom. Here we could see two very interesting functions performed by this narrative. In the first place, the process of composition of an event is specific and internal to the characters and their categories. Second, it joins together and synthesizes the triple distinction in the form of exposition, resolve and resolution.

## IX

In *The Pilgrim's Progress* the strength of narrative is hidden not in an individual rather in the internal and external categories which determine the existence of man in this world. Christian, the central character, and the minor forms like Pliable, Interpreter, Athiest and the like enter into an opposed equative principle. Christian is an individual yet he does not have capacity to project himself as a medium, content and even the context. For this reason, the worth of communication is sometime lost and sometime dispersed, whenever the situation of crisis is authenticated by intensity of perception. At the beginning, Christian vows to approach the truth by submitting himself to the necessity of displacement. In fact, Christian develops a method through which he could revive an intensity of a category, let us say thought or imagination to activate a ground for his stay in a rather compulsive position. The external determinants like worldly constraints, temptations and illusions do not allow him to approach a movement along a path that is obtained through great difficulty. Christian's displacement from beginning of the situation has equal and parallel regression.

In fact, the suitability of the whole is hardly accounted for in the generation of meaning in this narrative. The theme presented by John Bunyan is opted in election of finer principle in which the power of virtue and strength of virtue both have an equivalent effect and Christian goes on to enact suitable gestures for affirmation. The conditions are also quite not very helpful for a display of power and knowledge. Christian begins his movement through appearance as well as reality, and, on each account, he is caught by an illusion, nevertheless, the movement continues and the success is obtained right at the behest of failure. The construction of a theme could suggest how a category continues with the accomplishment of introspection and revision of truthful and real situation. It seems to be remarkable on the part of Bunyan to have introduced the idea of binary opposition between two distinct meanings corresponding to an opposition within Christian himself. Hence it is the Christian who could see the presentation of truth and its denial through strong and suggestive falsehood. It is not always pertinent to illustrate the developing meaning occupying various measures in a category yet the contradiction in the opposing paradoxes is quite befitting. The idea generated in the typical functional set-up is located and distributed through the eminence of character, and Christian's position is such that he could interact with a balance between the amount of displacement and the amount of regeneration and ideational position. In fact, it is only a play of ideology that conducts the progress of an action in this narrative with overwhelming authority. The journey of Christian inside and outside the hell till the gate of Heaven is really a marker of imperative for a category, say an experience that could resolve every infinite object into every finite meaning; for this reason every regression multiplies the power of generation and accordingly Christian in the Hell would mean an assurance of his possible arrival in the Heaven. The beginning and end (or the journey of Christian) bring about multiples of association and to complete the process, Christian is associated with Doubt, Atheist, Ignorance, on the one hand, Faith, Hope, Interpreter, Evangelist on the other. In each of these associations, Christian does not succeed in interacting with insignificance of value hence he commands a violence or attitude by being excessively burdened with an idea of evil. In that way, the displacement does not create a motive for any meaning as such. This appears to be one of the great technical problems that one faces while reading *The Pilgrim's Progress*.

## X

The structural units, obtained in *Jataka Tales* and *The Pilgrim's Progress*, invariably associate as a matter of necessity, the appearance, reality and illusion. These three assertive contents of the expanded category present nearly the total view of the semantic orientation observed in these two narratives. Appearance is a presentation in such a way that it is received and revolved directly to the object that has caused its inception. In *Jataka Tales*, the central character *bodhisattva* determines his individuality through unusual genitive and ablative markers. In genitive situation he could correlate the presentable form through effective communication. The effect of communication is obtained in equal measure in all the resolvable human forms. This proves the idea that *bodhisattva* is a perception whose figure is not only concentrated but consolidated through regular exposition, he makes in front of every possible human form that he comes across. In *Jataka Tales*, the method of characterization, the approach, have a similar groundwork. Perhaps it would be more appropriate to say that the action or the individual in which both linear and cyclical forms are obtained gain primacy. The individual form of *bodhisattva* is both receptive and idealistic. He could see the world through a divine perception. He could also associate himself with the individual beings that keep coming across him in order to get his help. The creation of reversibility in terms of communication is one of the great technical advancements that could be seen in *Jataka Tales*. *Bodhisattva* is relative to every perception inherent in an individual/a form/character that faces a crisis. In this context, the strength assumed by him is effectively a process of inclusive assertion. An individual in crisis claiming the Hell and *bodhisattva* in the capacity of divine figure, enriching the effect of both motive and reason in the individual, is a term of union in which inclusion plays an important role. Illusion is evidently a matter of finding worthlessness of meaning in an infinite situation. In the infinity, the position of both the object and the subject is randomly indeterminate and at the time of resolution, the reality of both the object and the subject becomes incomprehensible and inconclusive. Likewise in the narrative, illusory perception tends to deform the individual sanctity of the characters yet the truthful assertion does not allow the formation to become as such. This opposition between truth and unreality and indetermination brings forth the necessity of adopting a character through association and conjunction into the mould of refined functionality. The formation of attitudinal principle in relation to content and medium takes the shape of a thoroughgoing commitment.

## XI

How is it possible to say with authority and conviction that the narrative in *The Pilgrim's Progress* and *Jataka Tales* obtains a solid and firm groundwork of structure inasmuch as each of these narratives has a firm leaning for both the plot and characterization. The plots of these narratives are explicable through appearance and reality and even to an extent the presentation of illusion. The characters, in the second place, are introduced to ourselves through a generous commitment for truth, involvement, honour and universality. And, it is precisely because of this that *Jataka Tales* and *The Pilgrim's Progress* remain excellent in the entire range of fable narratives. The formation of meaning in consequence of the modification of individual/objects/characters/situations/events into their idealized/universalized form remains an occasion of greater emphasis and comprehension.

# Conclusion

THE formation of meaning in consequence of the modification of individuals, characters, objects, situations and events into their idealized and universalized forms remains an occasion of greater emphasis and comprehension. The nature of meaning is invariably in the form of an equilibrium that brings about a suitable presentation of internal and external forms in respect of canonical narrative events mentioned above. In the earliest narrative tradition of the East and the West, especially *Pañcatantra*, *Hitopadeśa*, *Kathāsaritsāgara*, *Siṁhāsana Battīsī*, *Betāl Paccīsī*, *The Decameron*, *Legends of King Arthur* and *The Canterbury Tales*, the nature of meaning is at once evident in the form of assured transmutation that is achieved either physically, verbally, emotively, materially, existentially or otherwise anthropomorphically. In either of the circumstances, the procedure that is significantly the order of perception is not only harmonious but realistic as well. The characters and events undergo a process of change and the nature of change is suggested and manifested in compatible union, incompatible association, profitable alliance and non-profitable cooperation. It would mean further that there is remarkably a lengthened systematization of every opposites. In fact, it would be better to say that the opposite gestural forms and linguistic constructs both are appropriately resolved so much so that the essence of union is expressed in the position of order obtained in each of the events. In these narratives, the significance of time, space and world at large is so exact that the interrelationship is enjoined upon the characters and their material function. Time and character, space and individual cohere around a cyclical invention in which the mutability and permanence of existence are invested in regular conformity to each other. Progress of the external world and the consummation of internal events are so complimentary and simultaneous that the evolution of object into event becomes almost a functional necessity. There are five principal orders of meaning which are of necessity, found in the process of resolution of narrative objects into narrative events. In order of hierarchy these forms of meaning are conjunction, injunction, conception, inception and comprehension.

The nature of meaning that is compulsorily evident in the first place is conjunction. In conjunction, the correlations, objects and variants, due upon the artistry in the narrations, enter into a complete ordering of systematic and methodical changes; hence conjunction is the first important movement that defines the basic circumstance of resolution of an objective into an event. In Indian narratives like *Pañcatantra* and *Hitopadeśa*, the harmony of figurativization is necessarily equal to the impending discourse, and, for that matter, both the internal and external components make a complete assortment of each other. The characters Bhairava, Gaṅgādatta, Damanaka, Sañjīvaka, Piṅgalaka, Bandhakī and others enjoin upon themselves such a vast extent of transformation that each ends up with a projected content. It would mean further that the emergence of an idea in the form of reality governs their figural appearance, and, accordingly, restore them in the form of conjunction. The value of each instance of appearance in the medium brings about a convincing beginning where the naturalization of form assimilates every other expression in the external world. In fact, we can say that the introduction of a character in the medium is so natural that it becomes capable of its own to invent a series of correlatives of its cyclical progression. The principal proposition that is fixed as a rule in Indian earliest narratives is the activation of complementary and successive idealization. In order to retain to be identified in the world, in which the material condition and circumstances are rather inharmonious, every character struggles to unify himself through appropriate correlatives. The length of struggle is conditionally beneficial because it upgrades the moral strength of the given character. Gaṅgādatta, for example, understands that he cannot promote the structural transformation of snake who is in a position to keep up himself simply for the reason that the scheme of life doesn't attend on the simplicity of experience, rather it is founded upon compelling, contending, paradoxical and contradictory material conditions. The keenness with which Gaṅgādatta restores the parameters of action is also an instance of contradiction in ethics and morality, which could be so successfully resolved. This is not limited to a narrative in *Pañcatantra,* rather as a rule it progresses and copes up with many individuals/forms/objects and the like. In each of the situations the strength is primarily hidden in the consequence which in turn is due upon a form hence the individuals and characters who come up to deal with the intrusion of material contents into ethical and moral principles beget larger events of comprehension. The invention of an idea to bring about necessary mutation of the scheme of life is one of the important phases of the growth of the character even in the circumstance of hardship, suffering, fraud, deceit, infidelity and the like; it continues to afford the sanctity of his rational conviction, in which the idea is always maturing to contain the critical composition of the experience, and, in that way, knowledge is appropriately constituted for resolution, and, also, otherwise for the general methods of bliss and happiness. In the individual, the inquisitive terms are compulsorily authenticated, thus he is not moved by any of the fallacies that is likely to come up during the course of his stay. In the general mechanism of life, the man, therefore, is one who conceives a commitment and disposes the concern for the sake of complete resolution. The qualitative conditions contained in the emergence of the best form of life are a sort of urge that compels the characters towards the significant assertion and the intensity of change that brings up the meaning precisely depend on such an identification. In the growth of meaning the proximity and cohesion were formed out of disparate existential and ideological circumstances, which become very important to commit one to dispose a crisis, born out of treachery, dishonesty and infidelity. The character, in the first place, dissociates him by professing almost ignorance yet it is always conscious and aware of the development which are taking place. To reform the erring spirit, it is always necessary to make him understand that there is no excess of deviant evasions. This results into the constitution of an equal magnitude of experience, imagination and the like. This equality in terms of categorical formation becomes a device to supplement the rational procedures to bring about total modification. The governing conditions, which are expressed in these narratives, are always held to be typically material in their immediate consequence, hence the hierarchy of truth, order, identity and reality is immanent almost at the speed at which the given character learns the ways of the world. Every sequence of experience is precisely so practical and real that it would never bear it to be cast off by any lengthening and prolongation of meditation. It insists upon the action which is as real as the truth and manifest identity. Causation of an action is the substance of reality that attends the ethical functions of the character or form. Even otherwise in the slightest and minimal disorganization of the order, the character would find it necessary and convenient to commit it to synthesizing the action so as to bring to an end the whole process. The intensity of participation moves the direction of the efforts and the enthusiasm is so well received and revived that evil or any contradictory proposition is entirely discredited. The events which find the true nature of resolution and conditions which govern the communication of evil are precisely at the points of a catharsis in that the action of good character would simultaneously be the revival of the environment that looms large in the background. The point of signification is obtained in the upgraded artistic situation that helps the character in introducing a set of reformatory measures to improvise the whole term and condition. In fact, it is the purification of the whole environment that governs the optimum conditions of meaning formation. In *Pañcatantra*, the narrative due upon Gaṅgādatta could well be taken as an instance. Gaṅgādatta is called upon to contrive for the sake of certain drastic reforms within the ethical form hence connives with a snake to get rid of the enemies. Towards the end, he comes to realize that generative conditions are almost heterogeneous in nature thus there is a need to homogenize them with certain advices from his wife. It reinvents the spatial procedures and seems to bring about the exact nature of a true ethical meaning that suggests the defeat of treachery and roguery. Between two similar or dissimilar characters, the bond of affirmation and denial are equally comprehended. Every character is in a position to presuppose a large extent of reality in which he seems to have discovered the identity of himself. Accordingly, evil is an evil only for those who are not in a position to understand the evilness of an evil. Thus, far from being a contrastive turn, it is most certainly the associative part of the discovery of the character. To be able to discover one in a congenial environment is the greatest effect of transforming event. It closes with a note on further intent in curiosity hence always puts apostrophic interrogative sign in which the representative character holds the sway. Thus snake in Gaṅgādatta's narrative insists on pursuits by claiming it as a condition of hospitality so much so that it cannot be contested, what is noted as apostrophic inquisitive mark afterwards opposes the resolution so vigorously and massively that the expansion of narrative is almost certainly recorded through the inquisitive accounts. The propriety of signification is concretized, and we can only wonder as to how and why a certain character with every conceivable evil and error on its side is in a position to convince those who claim better expression in the truth. The question very simply is not how to understand the opposition of truth and reality but it is related to a certain hierarchy of mutation that ultimately records the triumph of goodness. The discourses, on these events, proliferate the units of narrative and add to the maturing of action. The epistemology of knowledge that is realized with assured certainty in the inquisitive contents is also suggestive of a high degree of narrative growth. The emphasis has always been laid onto define the categories that is basically material condition of existence hence range in variation is very significant. A scholar, a teacher, a businessman, a worldly man, a farmer, a poor brāhmaṇa, a noble king, a wretched woman, an erring animal, a foolhardy lion, a shrewd jackal, a humble sparrow, each is a manifestation of a concrete principle of life. It may be good to the extent that it is a measure of change in the ethical and moral framework of behaviour or it may be altogether unworthy in that as it is supposed to unsettle the prescribed mode of behaviour. In assuming that the quality of action, the type of personality and the nature of attending environment are primarily best signified in the associative consequences inasmuch as generic properties to develop a sort of movement for composition. Two units, which could be identified as having the expressive and assertive properties, or also simultaneously brought together to maintain correlation with the next formative event in the hierarchal change. In these narratives signification is necessarily the most effective, first, in association, and, then, in contrast for the same reason. The cunning jackal, or fox, or a businessman, or a woman, or anybody else achieves a complete transmutation and the highest designation. It is so overwhelming that the virtuous functions seem to be losing the ground. Badness of the bad character is an expression of a success in resolution, in that it is retained for a very long period of time and expressly asserted to relegate the other possible concerns to the background. It would mean that in the process of transformation and association of the categories the contrastive models occupy different positions, and it would not be otherwise to say that association has a greater significance at the beginning than the contrast because it allows the character to substantiate, to concretize and to grow till the time it achieves its true meaning. In *Kathāsaritsāgara*, anxiety in morals is a primary turn of reduction and it grows almost entirely to the point of transformation by intending the characters to undo, outdo or overdo the losses in respect of the character, behaviour and the like. The reduction of the quantitative correlatives, which deform the reality of a truthful formation, becomes quite a realizable function that is convincing, persuasive and come to the strengthening of the situation. In *Kathāsaritsāgara*, commitment for a virtue and honour on the one hand, and remarkable defects in the character leading to disgrace and fall are compulsorily fitted into a scheme of signification, where mutual interdependence of one and the other is quite remarkable on the other. It is almost the extension of roguery that ultimately finds definite projection of virtue and the meaning, and definition of life is quite remarkable. In these narratives, life is seen as a movement from two complementary points at the extremes, where exchange of the losses of the benefits to the benefits and losses are regularly illustrated. A character learns the true meaning of life by suffering only in the hands of certain proven rogue markers and also by suffering a certain kind of exclusion, which is allowed into a general framework of life. In other words, the intersections of profit and loss are brought for competitive consideration at regular succession. The unit that primarily in the nearness of signification is inherent in the objects or situations which are completely identifiable. In Jātakas, the moral and ethical terms, appearing in their refined forms to the extent that each ultimately is suitably cognized in the harmony of *bodhisattva*. *Bodhisattva* is a condition of optimum transformation in that he diffuses, dissipates and organizes into one whole. The extent of organicity is the basis of one's start in the world and it also justifies, and in want of which interaction with the external world cannot take place. It begins with *bodhisattva* and comes to a close on him, and thus *bodhisattva* as an aggregate of all the units becomes a standard of meaning formation. In *Betāl Paccīsī* and *Siṁhāsana Battīsī*, the emergence of a comprehensible moral authority proposes to invent necessary function to standardize the significant ethical terms. In these two classes of narratives, identity of the character is by and large displaced by an important suggestive network, which obtains concretization by committed emphasis on transformation. The king, in both of the narratives, is an instrument of modification. He commences imperatives for social, cultural and moral reforms hence convenes a code of signification by identifying his own strength in every corresponding term. The basic methodology that engages the apparatuses of meaning generation is invariably based on the intensity of richness of refined sensibility in which the selection and combination of concrete factors give rise to harmony and conviction for the sake of an equally excellent life condition. As stated in the foregoing conjunction, injunction, conception, inception and comprehension become radical conditions to organize and situate functional motives so as to bring them to change in such way that every change is ultimately an occasion of a new shade of meaning.

## III

In the earliest Western narratives, the method and procedure to obtain meaning are primarily by the way of interpreting, suggesting and signifying the immediate exchanges between characters/form/events. In each of these, immediate exchange of characters responds to upgrade the identity of the pertinent reality, which allows them to become committed to the contents of necessary form hence the world in which the characters live is a world of order, accordingly, it would insist on an observance of order via optimum sincerity and commitment. The conjunctions which are so evolved are idealized in the signification of the material world in which every object is assertive, compulsive and focused upon the primacy of an immediate consequence. The models of conjunction work out a fine organization of every experience of the life, out of which some are illusive and the others are of necessity born out of instinctual curiosity. The characters promote in themselves an urge to subscribe to the formative or deformative standards enjoined upon them. In *The Decameron*, *The Canterbury Tales*, *Legends of King Arthur* and *The Pilgrim's Progress* opportunity is given to understand as to how and why the shift in instinct presupposes a form of instinct so much so that it destabilizes ethico-moral functions in the given situations. The act of modification, therefore, proceeds from heterogeneity and sums up the general meaning which may be brought to comprehension. In *The Decameron*, for instance, characters come to term with the decadence of the life by approaching compulsive sensory fallacies. The largeness of sensation, that is generally bodily and primarily focused on the condition of the lust, gives an occasion to them to introspect, meditate, muse and hence to recreate everything into a larger organic whole. Narrative composition, on that account, justifies the prolongation and durability of the correlatives, which are necessarily very expansive in nature. The two characters justifying the separate gender subscription opt for a curious alignment by intending a sin rather than by subsuming virtue. It would mean that every correlative appears first in the form of a paradox and proceeds to situate universality in the forthcoming contradiction, which are highly aggravated in nature. The arrangement of opposites, so arrived at, conduces to the model of meaning that is to be developed later. The narratives in *The Decameron* precisely aimed at performing activities of realization in which the object and the subject are nearly identified, designated and exposed. The adequate contents supported by rigid material frameworks are the ideal signifiers for the purpose. On that account, we would find that a man is intentionally deprived of a concern for virtue whereas the woman prescribes herself by making indulgences in the expressive conditions of her existence in the midst of these overbearing events. The process of modification is initiated no sooner than the proximity between man and woman is established. In *The Canterbury Tales*, similarly, the signifying functions are invested in the essential disposition of the given characters, accordingly, the Knight, Doctor of Physique, Wife of Bath, Summoner, Pardoner, Miller and the like are embodied in the reducing contents, where meanings are very explicit and ultimately become the centres through which projection of meaning is made. In *Legends of King Arthur*, the crisis in attitude is best observed in the virtuous fallacies, which are embodied in the knights of Arthur. *The Pilgrim's Progress*, also, likewise sees the universality in the committed reduction of the contents. The merit of Christian lies in the fact that he could overcome the paradoxes by generating substantial conjunctions, which, once again contradict the terms of presentation, yet he survives and emerges out of the crisis. In these narratives, therefore, the primacy is accorded to an invention inherent upon paradox so that a large body of conjunction could be obtained to idealize the artistic situation.

## IV

In the earliest Indian and European narratives, the configuration of meaning is, of necessity, a morphological process which depends largely on the expansion and reduction of the contents. The development of these two forms of procedural changes in the nature of the inherent categories ultimately brings about five principal instruments of transformation in the form of conjunction, injunction, conception, inception and comprehension. In each, this enrichment of correlatives, precision of events and adequacy of content finally prepare a ground for the emergence of a meaning that is almost universal in its primary significance.

# Bibiliography


Boccaccio, Giovanni, 1951, *The Decameron*, vol. I, tr. J.M. Rigg, London: The Navarre Society.

Bunyan, John, 1969, *The Pilgrim's Progress*, NewYork: Airmont Publishing Company.

Chaucer, Geoffrey, 1958, *The Canterbury Tales*, ed. Walter W. Skeat, Oxford: Clarendon Press.

Francis, H.T. (tr. & ed.), 1957, *Jataka Stories*, London: Luzac and Co.

Greimas, A.J., 1987, *On Meaning: Selected Writings in Semiotic Theory*, London: Frances Pinter.

*Hitopadeśa of Narayan Pandita*, tr. Pt. Rameshwar Bhatta, ed. Narayana Ram Acharya, Delhi: Chaukhamba Sanskrit Pratishthan, 2007.

*Kathāsaritsāgara* of Somdeva Bhatt, tr. Pandit Kedarnath Sharma, Patna: Bihar Rashtrabhasa Parishad, 1997.

Malory, Sir Thomas, 1996, *Le Morte D'Arthur*, ed. Tom Griffith, Hertfordshire, Wordsworth Classics of World Literature.

*Pālijātakāvalī*, tr. and ed. Pandit Batuknath Sharma, Benares: Master Khelarilal & Sons, Sanskrit Book Depot.

*Pañcantantra* of Viṣṇuśarmā, Sarala Hindi Ṭīkā of Gokuldas Gupta, Varanasi: Chowkhambha Vidyabhavan, 2006.

*The Jātakas*, vols I & II, ed. E.B. Cowell, tr. Robert Chalmers, London: Luzac & Company, 1969.

———, vols III & IV, ed. E.B. Cowell, tr. H.T. Francis & R.A. Neil, London: Luzac & Company, 1957.

———, vols V & VI, ed. E.B. Cowell, tr. H.T. Francis, London: Luzac & Company, 1957.

# Index